Change Management In A Week

Mike Bourne and
Pippa Bourne

First published in Great Britain in 2012 by Hodder Education. An Hachette UK company.

This revised, updated edition published in 2016 by John Murray Learning

Copyright © Mike Bourne and Pippa Bourne 2012, 2016

The right of Mike Bourne and Pippa Bourne to be identified as the Authors of the Work has been asserted by them in accordance with the Copyright, Designs and Patents Act 1988.

Database right Hodder & Stoughton (makers)

The *Teach Yourself* name is a registered trademark of Hachette UK.

British Library Cataloguing in Publication Data: a catalogue record for this title is available from the British Library.

Library of Congress Catalog Card Number: on file.

Paperback ISBN 978 1 473 60853 5

Ebook ISBN 978 1 444 15882 3

1

The publisher has used its best endeavours to ensure that any website addresses referred to in this book are correct and active at the time of going to press. However, the publisher and the author have no responsibility for the websites and can make no guarantee that a site will remain live or that the content will remain relevant, decent or appropriate.

The publisher has made every effort to mark as such all words which it believes to be trademarks. The publisher should also like to make it clear that the presence of a word in the book, whether marked or unmarked, in no way affects its legal status as a trademark.

Every reasonable effort has been made by the publisher to trace the copyright holders of material in this book. Any errors or omissions should be notified in writing to the publisher, who will endeavour to rectify the situation for any reprints and future editions.

Typeset by Cenveo® Publisher Services.

Printed and bound in Great B

John Murray Learning policy
recyclable products and mad
and manufacturing processe
regulations of the country of

John Murray Learning
Carmelite House
50 Victoria Embankment
London EC4Y 0DZ
www.hodder.co.uk

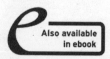
Also available
in ebook

Contents

Introduction

If an organization does not change in response to the environment in which it is operating, it will ultimately fail. Just as people have to change and adapt according to their circumstances, so do organizations. No one can deny that managing change is a difficult and sometimes painful task. It is complex and can be emotionally draining, involving a range of skills from project planning through to influencing those likely to be affected and ensuring that the appropriate actions happen. Difficult though it is, the ability to manage change is one of the critical skills needed by a manager. Anyone who wants to progress up the career ladder must be adept at instigating and managing change.

So what does managing change involve? Put simply, the four elements in the change process are:

1 Analysing the need for change and deciding what that change should be, based on your analysis
2 Planning and managing the change as a project or series of projects
3 Implementing the change and managing people through it
4 Ensuring that the change becomes well rooted so that it will continue to grow.

This book concentrates on the last two elements – implementing change and ensuring that it happens. It is designed to help managers overseeing the whole change and those who are managing part of the process and trying to keep it on track. It will also interest people caught up in the change process, helping them to understand why certain things are happening to them.

First, however, it is worth taking a quick look at why organizational change so often fails. John Kotter of Harvard Business School found eight common mistakes from his experience with change initiatives in over 100 different companies:

1 Not creating enough sense of urgency at the outset: if people do not know why change is required, they will not be committed to it

2 Failing to 'take people with you': you need commitment from powerful people

3 Underestimating the power of vision: create as tangible a picture of the future as you can so people see what you are trying to achieve

4 Being inconsistent in the way you act and thus undermining your own position

5 Permitting obstacles to remain and block progress: you must identify these and be seen to be overcoming them

6 Failing to create short-term wins to demonstrate success and to give people a chance to celebrate

7 Claiming success too soon: while it is tempting to announce the change is complete, if you do this too soon you may find it never becomes truly embedded

8 Neglecting to anchor the change securely in the corporate culture: to make it stick, it has to become 'the way we do things around here'.

Each day we will examine one aspect of managing change and at the end of each chapter you will find a set of questions to enable you to check what you have learned.

At the end of the book you will find a 'Checklist for change', which will provide a useful summary of the ideas presented in this book.

Mike Bourne and Pippa Bourne

SUNDAY

Why change is necessary

The phrase 'managing change' can sound vague. It is not like managing the implementation of a new IT system, where you can physically see different hardware and software, although that may in itself be part of a change management initiative. Managing change usually boils down to persuading people to operate in a different way, whether that is working with new equipment, within a new structure or with a different set of processes. It helps to think through what you are doing and why you are doing it in as concrete a way as possible. If you do that, you will be better able to avoid the pitfalls. More positively, the clearer the picture you have of what you are trying to achieve and what that will involve, the more you will be able to gain the commitment of others to your plans.

In today's chapter we will try to make the management of change more tangible to help you to 'get a handle on it'. We will look first at why change is necessary, then we will examine different types of change and a number of approaches to managing it. Finally, we will introduce you to the stages of the change process.

Must there be change?

Most people have experienced change at some stage in their working lives. This might be anything from the type of major change much reported in the media – downsizing, restructuring – to changes in job role resulting from the introduction of new technology. But is all this change *really* necessary?

There are some who say that change is important for change's sake. Without it, organizations and individuals become complacent and stale. At the other end of the spectrum, too much rapid and constant change brings its own problems, such as lack of loyalty among the workforce and loss of important skills and knowledge from the business when people leave. So why is change necessary? Of course, there are many reasons.

Increased competition means that if you do not continually analyse what is happening in your market, and change and improve what you are doing, then you will probably be put out of business.

Customers are demanding higher standards. In most cases customers have a choice about where they buy products or services and this leads to greater expectations of both. If they do not like what you offer, they can go elsewhere. This is the case even in instances where choice is not always so evident, such as in the UK's National Health Service, where people are demanding new drugs or treatments that they have read about and they are looking for the very best care.

Success and growth inevitably bring about the need for change. The profitable micro-business starts to employ more people; these people bring new ideas and experience that they want to use; communication becomes more complex as more people join the business; new machinery has to be brought in to cope with demand; and so it goes on.

Market decline nearly always heralds major change. This is not just downsizing and restructuring. It is also about the search for new and better markets, new and better ways of doing things.

Environmental factors beyond one's control can also force change. Wide variation in exchange rates can cause significant upheaval. New legislation on working hours, health and safety, and even the introduction of new tax regimes, bring change in their wake.

All this means that dramatic speedy change is bound to be necessary at some stage. In fact, it is often a single blow that acts as a driver for change – such as the loss of a very big customer.

> **'It is not the strongest species that survive, nor the most intelligent: it is the one most adaptable to change.'**
>
> Charles Darwin

The same is true of organizations.

Types of change

Changes come in all shapes and sizes but it is worth considering change along the following dimensions:

- Incremental change or radical change
- Continuous improvements or step change
- Participative or directed change.

Incremental versus radical change

Incremental change is the type of change you see occurring through continuous improvement. The steps are small but over time they become cumulative and the change can be significant.

Radical change, however, is very visible. This type of change often results from benchmarking or business process re-engineering exercises and involves a single significant step change.

Continuous improvement versus step change

Continuous improvement is used in many industries to develop the business. It has the advantage of breaking down changes into myriad smaller steps, each in itself easily achievable and delivering better performance. It is a low-risk strategy, which has the advantage of making change a constant process, thus eliminating the disruptive elements associated with many larger (or step) changes.

Continuous improvement is not a utopia. With the speed of change in industries, it is becoming more important to make step changes in performance improvements, which a continuous change approach often cannot deliver in the time available. Furthermore, breakthrough improvements in performance cannot always be developed from the existing methods of working; occasionally, a totally fresh approach is required.

	Benefits	Weaknesses
Continuous improvement	• Many small steps • Makes change habitual • Less disruptive • Lower risk • Creates cumulative gains	• Slow • May create tunnel vision and missed opportunities
Step change	• Stimulates radical thinking • Potentially quick gains	• Greater risk • Disrupts performance during the change

Consequently, continuous improvement is a good habit to foster in your business, but the rapidly changing business environment means that the ability to make step changes is an important technique to master and to apply effectively.

Participative versus directed change

There is much written these days about participative change, where those directly affected by the change are at least consulted on, if not fully involved in, formulating and managing the change themselves. Participative change relies on the goodwill of those involved in the change to work through the change process.

However, much change is still directed. When a car manufacturer decides to close a manufacturing plant, the workers may be consulted but rarely is the decision reversed. Directed change relies on those making the change having the power to order others and to make the change happen.

Participative change has caught the attention of many change agents because it fits well with our values and builds on employees' commitment and loyalty to the organization. However, there are circumstances, such as on a battlefield, where it is inappropriate and where more decisive action is needed.

Hard systems approach to change

This is the logical approach to change that is often adopted. The approach starts with decision making by asking the questions:

- What is the problem?
- What are the alternatives?
- Which alternative gives the best solution?

Once the decision has been made and the best alternative selected, the task is then one of implementation using standard project management techniques. This is illustrated by an example below:

Example: Developing new production capacity

Problem definition	
Current situation	• Market demand will outstrip capacity by next year
Constraints	• The new capacity has to fit within the existing building • The new capacity has to be available 1 January • Capital expenditure must have a two-year payback • Quality and availability must not be compromised
Objectives	• 30% increased capacity • 10% cost reduction
Option evaluation	
Options available	• Buy new machines • Upgrade existing line • Implement a night shift • Buy in the required capacity
Options discarded	• Buy new machines as two-year payback not possible • Night shift as local labour shortage
Preferred option	• Upgrade existing line
Decision	• Upgrade of existing line approved • Implementation
Project plan	• Timescales, resources, people
Resources	• Capital allocation agreed • External contractors appointed
Responsibilities	• Project manager appointed • Service teams agreed timescales • Production manager agreed implementation
Project manage	• Review progress against plan

This approach is widely used in managing change, but it makes certain assumptions:

● The nature of the problem is clear and unambiguous.
● The objectives and constraints can be clearly identified and stated.
● The alternatives can be generated by those involved.
● The selection can be made rationally against the criteria identified.
● Others agree with the assessment and will go along with the decisions made.

The TROPICS test

McCalman & Paton (1992) in their book, *Change Management: A Guide to Effective Implementation*, developed a test to assess changes into hard and soft complexity. Hard changes can be managed using the framework above (although you should always be on the lookout for the possibility of the situation developing into a more complex problem), while soft changes are more difficult to manage because of the social and emotional consequences of the change.

In practice, major change usually includes a mixture of hard and soft changes and the statements in the table below are at either end of a continuum. However, they do provide a useful framework against which to consider various stages of your change project.

Situations that are predominantly classified as hard are much easier to manage. Soft changes are more messy. They require much more recycling between the problem, its definition and the proposed solutions. The questions move from 'What should be done?' to 'Who should be involved?' The stages are no longer connected to making the decisions related to the change, but focus on making the change happen in the organization.

Test	Hard	Soft
Timescales	Clearly defined, short to medium term	Difficult to define, medium to longer term
Resources	Clearly identified	Unclear
Objectives	Clearly identified and stated	Subjective and ambiguous
Perception	The problem is perceived in the same way by all	The problem is seen differently by different people and groups, possible conflicts of interest
Interest	Interest in the problem known to be limited to a defined group	Interest in the problem is widespread or ill-defined
Control	Control of the problem can be kept to a managing group	Control of the problem is shared because of the influence of others
Source	The source of the problem originates within the organization	The source of the problem is external to the organization

Most changes fail because the soft aspects of change are not properly managed. It is these softer aspects which are now the focus of the rest of this book.

Stages in the change process

Half a century ago Kurt Lewin identified three major stages of change: 'unfreezing, moving and refreezing'. Although more complex models have been developed since, the three stages are still appropriate today.

Unfreezing

Unfreezing is the stage in which the organization prepares for change. A recognition of the need for change has to occur, alternatives are identified and a proposed course of action is selected. In addition to these planning activities, action must be taken to 'unfreeze' existing attitudes and behaviours in order to allow the change to occur. This stage is essential to generate support for the change initiative and to minimize resistance.

Moving

Moving occurs during the stage in which the new systems and procedures are implemented. Usually, this requires changes in organizational structures and processes, as well as the development of new behaviours, values and attitudes. Achieving this during a short period, when all the focus is on the change, is relatively simple compared with trying to sustain the changes in the longer term, hence the need for the third stage – refreezing.

Refreezing

During refreezing, action has to be taken to reinforce the changes that have occurred and to ensure that the new ways of doing things become habitualized or, as Kotter would put it, embedded in the organization's culture. Recently, critics have claimed that refreezing is inappropriate; in today's volatile markets, change needs to be ongoing. But most change efforts fail because people revert to their old ways rather than because they are stuck in the new ones.

TIPS

- *Logical analysis of the situation and the approach to managing change is vital but remember the social and emotional consequences that will throw plans into chaos and affect the outcome significantly.*
- *Identify which elements in the change are 'hard' and which are 'soft' and manage them accordingly.*
- *Don't narrow down options too early; think broadly for as long as possible about issues and possible outcomes.*
- *Be realistic about timescales and allow some slack; a list of missed deadlines makes a very bad impression.*
- *Implementation of change is not the final stage. When considering timescales and action plans, allow for continual monitoring against a set of criteria to ensure that changes are really embedded and are delivering the required results.*

Summary

Today we have covered three elements to consider when planning a change. So before you get too far into the change process you should ask yourself:

First, is this an incremental change that will happen gradually over a period of time? Or is this a step change, where you will physically stop what you are doing one day and start a completely new way of working on the next day? Both approaches have advantages and disadvantages.

Second, how directive or participative are you going to be? Participation can build long-term commitment and loyalty, but it takes time to implement, time that you may not have.

Third, have you decided whether you are going to take a hard systems approach to change or a soft systems approach? This is a decision you can take only once you truly understand the nature of the change you are embarking upon.

So today we have explained why change is necessary and presented the different types of change. Over the next three days we will take you through Lewin's three phases of change in more detail, unfreezing, moving and refreezing.

SUNDAY

MONDAY

TUESDAY

WEDNESDAY

THURSDAY

FRIDAY

SATURDAY

Fact-check (answers at the back)

1. Which of the following is true?
   a) Organizations are surviving longer ❏
   b) The need for change is reducing ❏
   c) Companies are failing at a faster rate ❏
   d) Change is easy to achieve ❏

2. Without change, the demise of your organization ...
   a) Is unclear ❏
   b) Is inevitable ❏
   c) Is possible ❏
   d) Will never happen ❏

3. Why does change fail?
   a) Through complacency ❏
   b) Through lack of vision ❏
   c) Through failure to communicate ❏
   d) All of the above ❏

4. Why would you adopt continuous improvement as a change strategy?
   a) It is low risk ❏
   b) It is quick to implement ❏
   c) It is the best approach ❏
   d) It delivers breakthrough results ❏

5. Why would you attempt a step change?
   a) To reduce risk ❏
   b) To avoid disruption to performance ❏
   c) It is the best approach ❏
   d) To deliver breakthrough results ❏

6. Soft systems approaches are best for
   a) Simple problems ❏
   b) Small changes ❏
   c) Quick fixes ❏
   d) Complex change initiatives ❏

7. Hard systems approaches are best for
   a) Simple problems ❏
   b) Situations where many people are affected ❏
   c) Cultural change ❏
   d) Complex change initiatives ❏

8. A participative approach to change is better than a directed approach:
   a) Always ❏
   b) Usually ❏
   c) Sometimes ❏
   d) Never ❏

9. Most changes fail through
   a) Lack of planning ❏
   b) Lack of direction ❏
   c) Lack of attention to the soft aspects of change ❏
   d) Lack of attention to the hard aspects of change ❏

10. According to Lewin, how many phases to change are there?
    a) 2 ❏
    b) 3 ❏
    c) 4 ❏
    d) 5 ❏

MONDAY

Unfreezing: creating the impetus for change

On Sunday we looked at types of change and various approaches to handling change. Now we will look at the signals that indicate change is necessary, at how you initiate that change and at a few of the problems you might encounter.

It is usually easier to accept the status quo – especially when things appear to be running smoothly – than to make changes. However, it pays to be bold and no organization is sustainable without evolving. It is invariably better to scan the environment and identify changes that may be necessary, even if only at some point in the future, than to have them thrust upon you at short notice with insufficient time to plan.

It is one thing to understand the need for change yourself but quite another to persuade others that it is needed. While you probably won't be able to persuade everyone, you do need to gather some supporters and we will pay particular attention to that in this chapter.

> *'There is nothing more difficult to plan, more doubtful of success, nor more dangerous to manage than the creation of a new system. The initiator has the enmity of all who would profit from the preservation of the old institutions and merely lukewarm defenders in those who should gain by the new ones.'*
>
> Niccolò Machiavelli, *The Prince*

A step into the unknown

Most people like working within their comfort zone. There is comfort in familiarity and routine, and in knowing that you are competent at what you do. Even those people who say they are looking for 'a challenge' have limits beyond which they may fear to go.

Change, for both the initiator and those affected, is rather like a journey into the unknown. You cannot predict accurately how people will react or how new processes and procedures will work. For those subject to change, there are many questions, and often fears that they do not know the whole story. They may worry that senior managers have a hidden agenda and that things may, in fact, be far worse than they appear.

Initiating and working with change is such a difficult issue, so how do you create the impetus for it to happen?

In many cases, the need for change is obvious – a downturn in the market, a new competitor or some political influence, perhaps. In these cases everyone is aware that 'something needs to happen'. At first sight this may seem a good starting point – the need for action is clear so there should be less resistance. In fact, this is not necessarily true.

Major change forced on the organization at the last minute can mean the whole project has been rushed through with too many hurried decisions, exceptions made for political expediency and no time to think through the consequences. From the viewpoint of those subject to the change – even if they know it is necessary – they still have the same fears and concerns.

Avoiding the panic response

It is important, then, to avoid last-minute change projects that can leave everyone battered and bruised. This comes back to some basic strategic actions:

- **Keep in touch with what is happening at every level of the organization:** those working at the sharp end, dealing with customers, clients or patients are often the first to detect trends and usually have a realistic view of the situation.
- **Look forward:** it is easy to be wrapped up in the present and to be absorbed in the infallibility of your own product and service. Think about the true story of the slide rule manufacturer who continued to make better and better slide rules and failed to notice the arrival of the calculator!
- **Monitor your competitors:** keep in close touch with your customers.

This does not mean 'analysis for paralysis', but it should help to predict when change is likely to be necessary and provide some time for thinking and planning.

Some danger signals

The signs that change will be necessary are often present for some time but pass unnoticed because all appears to be going well. The following are some typical danger signals:

- **Managers believe all is well.** The company is not losing money so everything is all right. The UK-based company Marks & Spencer might have been in this situation in the mid-1990s. Profits were the best they had ever been, but customer satisfaction was falling. It was not until sales were hit that the problem became serious, and the company has been working hard to rebuild its reputation and sales ever since. Latest figures indicate that they have been very successful at this.
- Another frequently quoted danger signal is having **too many symbols of success.** The palatial head office building, expensive furniture and thick carpets are all examples, but so are pictures in the *Financial Times* and *Forbes* magazine.
- **Low performance standards** lead to almost inevitable failure. This often comes from a lack of external comparison – the company may think it is performing well but actually it is not. An example of this is when a company is suddenly shocked to find when its patent protection runs out that competitors are selling their product at prices below their manufacturing cost.
- **Inappropriate performance standards** are also dangerous. Standards are sometimes set because they are easy to measure and achieve, rather than being appropriate.
- Some companies find that they are **too functionally based** or **too hierarchical** to allow the flexibility and speed of working needed to compete. Painful restructuring is often necessary.
- **Arrogance** is a major problem. In the Probe benchmarking studies run by IBM and the London Business School, it was seen that the very best companies were nearly always concerned that they were not as good as the competition (a form of corporate paranoia), whereas the merely good companies deluded themselves that they were better than everyone else.

'Burning platforms'

As we saw earlier, according to John Kotter, not creating enough urgency at the outset is the first most common mistake in trying to implement change. Creating a 'burning platform' is one way of generating the sense of urgency.

The burning platform analogy comes from an oil rig disaster in the North Sea. One of the people involved described the decision he had to make: jump over 30 m (100 feet) into the sea and any other unseen obstructions under the water, something he had been systematically trained not to do, or stay on the platform with the fire. The pressure of the fire was eventually so great that he jumped. Luckily, he was found in the water and rescued.

In business terms, creating a burning platform is forcing the organization to make a choice, to do something quickly that it would not naturally do at all. How is this done?

- Emphasizing a bad financial result is one way. By judicious use of stock write-off, contingencies and other financial techniques, a poor performance can be exaggerated for effect. The loss of profit will often create a shock.
- Projecting future trends is another way. If you are losing market share, any ten-year prediction will show a very depressing future.
- Create an ogre of a competitor, using the loss of business to one competitor in one segment as an example of what may happen to the whole business.

Case study: Philips

Shortly after becoming CEO of Philips in the mid-1990s, Jan Timmer needed to get the attention of the senior management team of the company and communicate the seriousness of the situation they faced. He called a meeting of the 100 most senior executives in the company and handed out a hypothetical press release announcing the bankruptcy of the corporation. This proved to be the first step in a turnaround of the financial fortunes of the business, increasing the share price by 150 per cent over the next four years.

Case study: Svenska Handelsbanken

Similarly, soon after taking control as President of Svenska Handelsbanken, Dr Jan Wellander had a problem communicating the serious nature of the company's under-performance. The bank was well established and very traditional in its approach and, although profitable, was not performing well. Wellander cancelled the bank's centenary celebrations and suddenly he had everyone's attention.

Burning platforms are, therefore, an important tool in unfreezing, creating the impetus for change.

The change formula

Is there a magic formula for implementing change?

Change by its very nature is messy – it is difficult to manage and control. The bigger the change, the messier it usually becomes, so there is no magic formula. However, David Gleicher, a consultant at Arthur D. Little, proposed one very useful method of looking at change in the 1960s. His argument was that organizational change would occur only when dissatisfaction with the current situation, the desirability of the future goal and the knowledge of the first step to get there combine to outweigh the costs involved. This was expressed in the form of a formula.

$$K \times D \times V > C$$

where:

    K represents **K**nowledge of first practical steps
    D represents **D**issatisfaction with the status quo
    V represents the desirability of the **V**ision of the future
    C represents the **C**ost, both material and psychological, of doing something.

The multiplication signs in this formula are included to represent how the factors combine. It also means that if any single factor is missing (i.e. the value of that factor reaches zero), the change will not occur.

The formula can also be used as a checklist. For example:

● Are we all really unhappy with the current situation?
● Do we have a consistent and shared view of where we want to be?
● Do we know what the first actions are to move forward?
● Have we calculated the true cost (both material and psychological) of making the change?

The change formula also emphasizes the importance of communication, especially the realities of the current situation and the vision of the future.

Managing the communication

Communication is like the oil in a machine. Without it, all the parts grind to a halt: put in the wrong oil and the result is similar; let the oil get into places where it should not be and you have a serious problem.

Ensuring effective communication is important at every stage of the change process but it is particularly important at the beginning. What happens at this stage will set the scene for future stages of the project.

There are several critical issues to be considered:

How open should you be?

This will depend on the situation – clearly, there are some situations where you cannot be open. However, the general rule is to tell people as much as possible – taking them into your confidence will help to build trust. In any case, most people are not stupid and will guess what is happening.

The degree of openness will depend on what you are trying to achieve. There are cases where it is better to let bad news seep out slowly because you cannot afford a sudden adverse reaction such as the resignation of key individuals.

What methods of communication should you use?

In most cases the more personal the communication the better. Email, letter, video are rarely appropriate. Communication implies a two-way process, and being face to face with people enables you to gauge their reaction and to dispel misunderstandings much faster.

All the normal rules of communication still apply. Different groups of people will respond better to different approaches. Some may want one-to-one meetings; others will want facts and figures; some will want to take away information to read. However, the key points that everyone will want to know are:

- What are the changes?
- Why are they happening?
- What will the end result be?
- What will it mean for me?

The difficulty is that the most important of these questions (the last) is also the most difficult to answer. In fact, the answer may not be known in the early stages of the change process. The best approach is to be straightforward. Show an understanding of how people feel, show an appreciation of the uncertainty but keep a positive stance.

How do you control communication?

You can manage and control only part of the communication. You cannot directly control the grapevine – and email makes it so easy to copy dozens of people instantaneously into views that the author might later regret. The key here is to keep an ear open to what is being emailed or gossiped about.

The other element of controlling communication is to keep a record of what has been said at meetings and to ensure that, when an issue has been agreed, it is recorded in unambiguous terms.

TIPS

● The earlier you identify the need for change, the less painful it will be.

● In the course of creating dissatisfaction with the present, be sure to look after your key people; good employees are hard to replace and you will need their skills and experience throughout the change process.

● Keep meticulous records of meetings; writing draft minutes and sending them out is often a good way of gauging depth of feeling.

● Without being too manipulative, take certain people into your confidence and ask them to provide feedback to you about what is being said behind your back.

● Create a communication plan for the whole project. Although effective communication is critical at the early stages, it is easy to forget to communicate later on when you are deeply embroiled in myriad actions.

Summary

Most large organizations become complacent at some time or another. They can miss the change in the marketplace and suddenly business starts to slip away. This slip may not be seen by all so the organization may be slow to react.

Creating a burning platform is a good first step. Creating a burning platform makes the need to change a reality. But dissatisfaction with the status quo is not enough to create change. You will need a vision of the future and knowledge of how to take the first few steps to get there.

If the organization isn't ready for change, change won't happen. Unfreezing is therefore essential for successful change to occur. It helps to create the right conditions for the second stage, 'moving', which is the transition to where you want to go – the subject we will look at tomorrow.

SUNDAY

MONDAY

TUESDAY

WEDNESDAY

THURSDAY

FRIDAY

SATURDAY

Fact-check (answers at the back)

1. The need for change will always be ...
   a) Obvious to all ❏
   b) Readily recognized ❏
   c) Blatantly apparent ❏
   d) Recognized initially by only a few ❏

2. The earlier the need for change is identified
   a) The better ❏
   b) The more confusion occurs ❏
   c) The more costly the change ❏
   d) The harder it is to manage ❏

3. Which of the following is not a danger sign?
   a) Arrogance ❏
   b) Strong functional controls ❏
   c) External benchmarking ❏
   d) Symbols of success ❏

4. Panic responses to changes in the environment should be ...
   a) Expected ❏
   b) Encouraged ❏
   c) The rule ❏
   d) Avoided ❏

5. The first phase in any change project should be ...
   a) Blind panic ❏
   b) Making the change ❏
   c) Unfreezing ❏
   d) Ignoring the need to change ❏

6. Creating a 'burning platform' should ...
   a) Cause panic ❏
   b) Create a sense of fear ❏
   c) Cloud the issues in smoke ❏
   d) Create a sense of urgency ❏

7. Change requires ...
   a) A vision ❏
   b) Dissatisfaction with the status quo ❏
   c) A knowledge of the first steps to take ❏
   d) All of the above ❏

8. Communicating to the staff through a change project is ...
   a) Best avoided ❏
   b) Optional ❏
   c) Important ❏
   d) The only thing that matters ❏

9. Communication during a change project should always be done ...
   a) Face to face ❏
   b) By email ❏
   c) By all means available ❏
   d) By rumour and gossip ❏

10. The key question for staff in a major change will be:
    a) Why change? ❏
    b) What will change? ❏
    c) When will change occur? ❏
    d) How will it affect me? ❏

TUESDAY

Moving: the change roller-coaster

On Monday we talked about preparing for change, which we have called 'unfreezing'. Today is all about moving, the stage when the change actually occurs. This is the stage when uncertainty really creeps in, both from the perspective of the initiator and from the perspective of those affected. The initiator may find that all is not going quite as expected – people who appeared to be 'on side' reacted negatively, perhaps, or systems did not work as they should.

Those affected by the change may react badly because it is dawning on them that the change is really happening and is affecting them personally. (It's quite easy to assume that you won't be affected by any changes, particularly if you have been with your company for a long time.)

This is the time when emotions are high and there is a danger that too much introspection affects the day-to-day running of the business, so it is important to keep what is happening in perspective.

In today's chapter, as well as looking at the change process from the point of view of those involved – as a manager it is important that you can see how others may be feeling about what is happening – we will look at different ways of working through it: collaboration, consultation and communication.

The recipient of change

Consider for a moment the last time you were confronted by a major change at work. Perhaps your boss suddenly resigned without warning; the company announced a reorganization, merging your department with another; or you received notice that your office was to close. What was your immediate reaction?

Most probably you were shocked, shaking your head in disbelief. This may then have given way to anger, 'Why is this happening?' and in particular 'Why to me?'

These responses are natural – people all respond to change in similar ways. However, those who initiate change often forget what it is like to be on the receiving end of the change. Then they are surprised at the reaction of those affected by the change. Why is this? From the point of view of the one initiating change:

> *'The change is only small, we know that nobody will lose their jobs and the reorganization will create so much more efficiency. There will be a reallocation of tasks and reporting, but they will get used to it in a few days.'*

But for the recipients it is often change that they do not want and cannot control:

> *'The change looks large, management are saying there will be no job losses but with all these efficiency gains I don't really believe it. The work will be different, and I am not sure I will enjoy the new set-up as much as the old. Will I be working with my friends? Am I going up or down in the pecking order? What about that pay rise/promotion I was promised at my last appraisal?'*

Those facing change have so many more unanswered questions, depending on their own particular situation and circumstances. The way to manage change effectively is to understand this and the roller-coaster on which staff are about to embark. In this way, you can plan for the more obvious difficulties and not be surprised by people's reactions.

The change roller-coaster

THEY SURVIVED THAT, NOW LET'S SEE IF THEY MANAGE THE JUMP!

Many people have written about the 'change roller-coaster', as the result of both research and experience. We will describe two similar approaches. The first relates to changes in performance and self-esteem (see Figure 3.1).

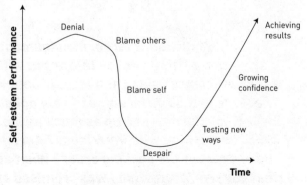

Figure 3.1 The change roller-coaster (adapted from Carnall 1995)

Some would argue that the change in performance slightly lags behind the change in self-esteem, but the graph looks very similar. The roller-coaster starts with denial: the change is unnecessary, the change will never happen, the change will never work. People then blame others for the need for change, they blame themselves for not seeing it coming and getting out of the way, and they end up in the depths of despair. Eventually, the change cannot be ignored. Gradually, people start to test what they can do and, through trial and error, develop new ways of working and the new team starts to form. As this happens, confidence grows and performance rises.

The second approach relates to the type of emotional response, passive or active (see Figure 3.2), and has eight distinct phases:

1 The **initial situation** preceding the announcement of the change is neutral and represents the status quo.
2 **Immobilization** follows. This is as a result of shock, as those facing unwanted change are disoriented and confused.
3 **Denial:** the change is rejected or people try to ignore it.
4 **Anger:** the change will not go away and denial turns to anger caused by hurt and frustration. People lash out at those around them.

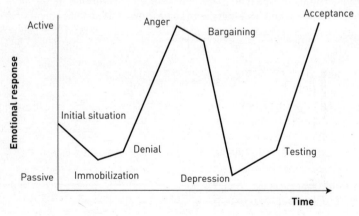

Figure 3.2 Emotional responses to negative change (adapted from Connor 1992 © ODR)

5 **Bargaining:** individuals realize that the change cannot be avoided, so they start to bargain to minimize the negative impact. This may be in terms of extensions to deadlines, requests for clarifications or transfers to a new position. This represents the beginning of acceptance of the change.

6 **Depression:** individuals feel a sense of resignation, possibly a sense of helplessness in the face of the change. This leads to low levels of energy and lack of interest in the job. Emotionally, this phase is where the full negative impact of the change is recognized and accepted, and this helps the process of moving on.

7 **Regaining control** comes through testing and acknowledging the new way of working, while pushing the boundaries of what is allowed. This leads to the discovery of how to be successful under the new regime.

8 **Acceptance:** this does not mean that individuals like the new way of working, but that they accept the targets that have emerged and settle into a new form of normality.

Managing moving

Experience shows that change will be resisted and that managing the transition requires helping individuals through their personal change roller-coaster. This should include:

- Accepting the reaction to change and not being surprised by it
- Planning for the downturn in performance during the transition
- Providing information and support to those who need it
- Expecting the anger and apparently irrational response when it comes
- Negotiating realistically, giving way on those points which can be conceded, but not on those fundamental to the change
- Helping people to experiment with the new ways of working
- Setting targets and goals as the situation becomes clear, in order to give people the chance to be successful again.

Management's perceptions of change

So far today, we have considered the reactions to change of those subject to the change. However, there is another journey taken by those initiating the change – those who start with a positive view of what is being proposed.

Consider, for a moment, the last time you tried to make a change at work. You started off with good intentions and the benefits of the change were there for all to see. But then the change started to get difficult. Perhaps the systems you were using were not quite as flexible as you thought, staff found the change burdensome and did not co-operate. Suddenly, the benefits do not look as tempting as they did before. So what could you have done?

What we have just described is how people react when they implement change; they go from uninformed optimism to informed pessimism (see Figure 3.3). There are then two paths: opting out when the going gets too hard and continued progress.

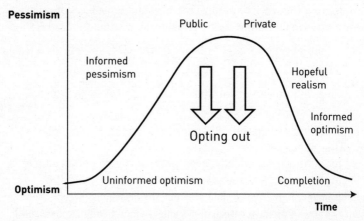

Figure 3.3 The initiators' response to change (adapted from Connor 1992 © ODR)

Opting out occurs quite often in change projects. Unlike the recipient of change, the initiator has the advantage of being able to abandon the change, and this is why many change efforts fail. People can opt out publicly, by announcing the end of the initiative, or they can do it privately, by simply letting the initiative slide and be overtaken by other events. The latter is seen more often in business, but means that the reasons for failure are never raised and discussed. A series of 'private opting outs' may lead, over time, to an organization becoming almost incapable of making changes.

When opting out does not occur, the next phase is hopeful realism. The difficulties are not overcome, but perhaps the change initiator can see a way of achieving their goal. When successful, this leads to informed optimism and the completion of the task.

The options for change

In designing change there are basically three modes of working:

1 Collaboration
2 Consultation
3 Communication.

Collaboration

Collaboration occurs when members of a team work together through a change programme. Obviously, not everyone in the team will have the same status or an equal say in what happens, but during collaboration the team work together to develop the plan and deliver the change.

Collaboration has a number of advantages:

● It creates an understanding of why the change is needed.
● It enables individuals with different experience and skills to become involved in the key change decisions.
● It builds a commitment to implementing the change.
● It creates a critical mass of people to help push the change through.

However, collaboration has its disadvantages:

- It takes time to create and build the team.
- There may not be consensus on the best course of action.
- The team, working on their own, can become isolated from the rest of the organization.

Consultation

Consultation occurs when the work of an individual or group is presented to others for acceptance, before it is implemented. This often occurs when external consultants are used, because their work should be scrutinized before it is implemented. It also occurs in democratic organizations where members are consulted, and it happens increasingly in more participative businesses.

Consultation has a number of advantages:

- It creates an understanding of why the change is needed.
- It enables alternative perspectives to be considered.
- It should reduce resistance to the change.

But consultation also has disadvantages:

- It takes time to undertake, especially with larger groups of people.
- Consultation does not necessarily mean the change will be accepted.

Communication

Communication occurs when people are informed of the change and have little or no say in what is happening. This approach to change is becoming less used in business, but is useful for crisis situations – probably the most obvious example of this is in a war situation. For simple communication to work, a degree of discipline and coercion is required. Just because the change is communicated, do not expect the change to be followed willingly.

Usually, the choice is not between these three options. The choice is who to involve in which aspects of the change and when. The following brief example will demonstrate this:

Example

A builder's merchant wanted to roll out a new performance management system across its branch network, but was concerned about how to ensure the buy-in of the different levels of the management team.

The project started with a small team who planned the initial approach. To gain support from the regional managers, these managers were given a day's education, along with the rest of the management team, on the theory and practice of the new approach. At the end of this session, an outline of what the company was trying to achieve was presented and the whole group discussed the change.

Following this launch, a steering team was created, enlarging the original project team by including other representatives. Over the next three months, the steering team met on a regular basis and fleshed out the new management system. On a monthly basis they went back and presented their findings to the regional managers, who discussed the plan and made suggestions. By this time, the change was ready for the larger management team and so a convention centre was hired and all the company's managers were invited and the project communicated.

This approach then continued as the project was developed and rolled out across the whole company.

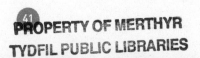

This example is included to show that the three approaches are not mutually exclusive, but you have to make a choice of *whom* to involve in *what* and *when*.

TIPS

- *Be prepared for the focus of the organization to turn sharply inwards; this can be of real concern if too many people become more concerned with what is happening internally rather than looking after their customers.*
- *Keep an open door so that people can express their concerns, but do not give way on important issues.*
- *The change is tough on the initiators as well as those on the receiving end of the change; be prepared for this.*
- *It can be helpful to build a support network among managers implementing the changes. This may involve scheduling regular but informal meetings of smaller groups (three to four people) to discuss how they have handled problems arising from the changes.*

Summary

Change is hard, both for the recipient and the initiator of the change. Each has their own journey and whether you are the initiator or recipient you should be prepared for the emotional roller-coaster ride.

In managing the change, you have a choice between collaborating, consulting and communicating. Each approach has its own advantages and drawbacks. But the critical question you must ask is 'Who do we involve in what and when?' Ask this question continually, until the change is demonstrably complete and well embedded in the working practices and culture of the organization.

During change, people often become internally focused and they obsess about things happening in the organization. This is dangerous as people lose sight of the bigger picture – what customers, competitors and the markets are doing. For organizations to survive, they must have the ability to change and adapt while still keeping an eye open for the next big issue; otherwise, they are always behind the competition.

So, by the end of Tuesday, the changes have been implemented. But beware: change has a nasty habit of unravelling. Embedding the change – or refreezing – is the subject for tomorrow.

SUNDAY

MONDAY

TUESDAY

WEDNESDAY

THURSDAY

FRIDAY

SATURDAY

Fact-check (answers at the back)

1. The first reaction to change is ...
   a) Anger ❏
   b) Blaming people ❏
   c) Denial ❏
   d) Performing ❏

2. During a change performance should be expected ...
   a) To increase ❏
   b) To remain roughly static ❏
   c) To decline ❏
   d) To be unpredictable ❏

3. During change you should negotiate but concede ...
   a) Nothing ❏
   b) To every request ❏
   c) Points that don't undermine the change ❏
   d) Only when necessary ❏

4. People making the change will need to ...
   a) Experiment with new ways of working ❏
   b) Do as they are told ❏
   c) Blindly follow the new processes ❏
   d) Wait for instructions ❏

5. During change people behave ...
   a) Totally rationally ❏
   b) Completely irrationally ❏
   c) Rationally from their own perspective ❏
   d) Unpredictably ❏

6. For the managers of the change ...
   a) There is no emotional engagement ❏
   b) It is emotionally demanding ❏
   c) It is an easy life ❏
   d) Their future is secure ❏

7. Consultation is ...
   a) The most collaborative form of change ❏
   b) Unhelpful ❏
   c) The only way to proceed ❏
   d) Helpful in reducing resistance to change ❏

8. Collaborative change ...
   a) Is quick and easy ❏
   b) Builds commitment to implement ❏
   c) Is always successful ❏
   d) Is the last resort ❏

9. Communicating a change ...
   a) Means everyone will follow ❏
   b) Doesn't mean people will follow willingly ❏
   c) Has no effect ❏
   d) Is a waste of time ❏

10. During change, people's concerns should be ...
    a) Ridiculed ❏
    b) Aired but then ignored ❏
    c) Hidden from senior management ❏
    d) Listened to carefully and acted upon appropriately ❏

WEDNESDAY

Refreezing: making the change stick

It is said that 'old habits die hard' and it is indeed surprising how difficult it is to shift them: they become ingrained; they become a comfortable and even automatic part of 'how things work'. You only have to think about your personal life: your route to work perhaps; just the way you do things. Even if you are shown a better route to work or a better way of doing something, you may be sceptical about adopting any new approaches until you have tried and tested them several times. When you see the new approaches are better, they will become new habits and you will feel comfortable with them.

So, if you are a manager implementing change, you need to ensure that the changes you make stick and become part of everyday working. It is too easy for old habits to creep back once the initial excitement and drive of the project is over.

In many organizations, you can see that people are paying lip service to the change but not fully engaging with it. In some cases, employees go to great lengths to find difficult-to-detect methods of sticking to old ways of doing things. Changes need to become habits.

Refreezing

The third stage of change is often called 'refreezing'. However, as change is becoming the rule, 'refreezing' is no longer considered appropriate because it is expected that further change will soon be required to move the business on again. Nevertheless, the change needs to be anchored in some way; otherwise, the benefits will be lost as the organization slips back into the old ways of working.

NOT QUITE YET

Today is about making the change stick. Ideally, the benefits of the new ways of working will be so self-evident to everyone that they will be owned and embraced by the whole organization. However, this rarely happens and, even if such a utopian situation is achieved, the company's systems will often undermine it.

Example

Take the example of a retailer selling equipment to the electrical trade. For many years each branch outlet had been treated as a profit centre, which focused the local managers' minds on running their own business. The side effect was that all the branches competed, not only with their competitors, but with each other. This was not good for the business as a whole, and everyone in the business knew that. But the competition continued until the recognition and reward system was changed. This removed the incentive for branches to compete with each other and the practice rapidly ceased.

Today, we will look at embedding the change through three perspectives:

1 Anchoring the change in the organization's structure
2 Anchoring the change in the organization's recognition and reward system
3 Anchoring the change in the organization's culture.

Anchoring the change in the organization's structure

This is one of the simplest and most effective ways of anchoring change and is illustrated by these examples:

Motor dealership acquisitions

A director did not have any problems integrating new garages into his motor dealership network. His approach was to dismiss all the existing employees, put in his own manager and recruit a completely new team. This way he was not burdened by all the old practices.

A distribution network company

A distribution company had a network of branches from which its fleet of lorries operated. To ensure the organization did not become ossified, the company had an unofficial policy of closing every branch after seven years. This was achieved by setting up new branches all the time and by moving work between the older branches and the new ones.

Again, the company could change ways of working and be unconstrained by past practices.

Turning performance around

A network repair organization had a national coverage in the UK. Poorly performing branches were supported by external help. However, if this proved too difficult, an alternative was to shut the branch and reopen with a new team. This could be achieved by moving the work through the national call centre to adjacent branches and reallocating the staff as well.

The branch could then be reopened some weeks later with a completely new team who were unconstrained by the old ways of working. This approach regularly provided spectacular results.

Designing the organization's structure

An American automotive components manufacturer was setting up a new manufacturing plant in Europe to supply two of the major car producers. Conscious of their past history and union problems in the United States, they decided to adopt a radical approach for the new plant. To achieve an extremely high level of customer focus, they built the plant with two production lines, each serving one of the two customers. Although the two lines were located on the same site, there was a separate management team for each and minimal shared services. Each plant then totally focused on serving its own customer without the normal internal wrangling the company had been used to dealing with. There were additional costs because now there were two distinct management teams, but these were more than compensated for in customer service and productivity.

Unfortunately, one of the plants lost its business in a downturn. The company's response was to simply shut that production line. This was achieved in days, whereas under the old structure, a similar problem in the States would have taken months to resolve.

As you can see from these examples, managing through structure can be a highly effective way of changing performance. It is also very brutal, but with falling trade barriers and global competition, it is becoming increasingly easy for large companies to manage performance in this way.

Take recent plant closures in the UK, such as Ford's 2012 closure in Southampton. These change an industry. Even when the closure is not made, as with Vauxhall's Ellesmere Port plant, the threat of taking work elsewhere creates a burning platform enabling rapid change.

Changing the structure and reporting can embed change. It immediately highlights where the problems are occurring, where there is resistance, and this allows management to focus their effort precisely on the point where it is needed. However, not all change can be managed through structure. Here are the alternative approaches.

Anchoring the change in the organization's recognition and reward system

One of the main reasons why change initiatives do not stick is because the support systems are not aligned with the change. When a change is implemented, the support systems, including incentives, recognition, reward and performance measures, should at least be neutral to the change. Too often these systems act against the change. To really drive the change forward, the systems should be aligned to the change.

There are two questions to ask:

- If you were measured using the existing performance measures, how would you behave?
- Is this behaviour supportive of the new way of working?

Similar questions arise with incentives, recognition and reward:

- If you were rewarded using the existing reward system, how would you behave?
- Is this behaviour supportive of the new way of working?

If, in each case, the answer to the second question is 'no', then the measurement and reward systems need to be realigned with the change.

Alignment: an example

A national repair service company spent two years designing and implementing a new performance measurement system, which they rolled out to their branch managers. At the end of the roll-out, they had achieved some extra focus on the specific aspects of the business, but the expected improvement across the board did not happen. Part of the reason for this was that the operatives were still paid on a flat-salary basis. The way they maximized their pay was through working overtime, which was expensive for the company and did not benefit the business or the customer.

The company then changed the practice and effectively abolished overtime. Operatives were paid a fixed wage, but additional earnings came from completing additional jobs over the average required. This new bonus system drove increased productivity because operatives were given incentives to increase the number of jobs they completed in a week. This encouraged the same out-of-hours support for the customers that the business required, but at a lower cost. It also improved overall productivity and profitability.

The company was also concerned about the quality of workmanship. Therefore, the incentive scheme included a penalty for repair; the operative whose job required rectification lost the bonus for that work. Thus, the performance measurement and incentive schemes were closely aligned to the company's objectives of improving productivity while not compromising the customer service or quality of the work.

Whatever the change in the organization, the incentive system should be reviewed to ensure alignment. This is often a forgotten step and a major source of change failure.

Anchoring the change in the organization's culture

The third method of anchoring the change is to combine hard change with a change in the organization's culture. This is by far the most difficult type of change to achieve – creating organization culture is a book in itself – but when it does occur, the change can be most profound and widely owned and accepted.

Aligning the structure and incentive systems are an initial first step; the rest comes from the values of the senior management team, often handed down from the original founders and perpetuated by successive generations of management.

ARE YOU SURE WE'VE WON?

Changing the culture

Occasionally, in a major crisis, cultural change occurs quickly. After the bankruptcy of a machine tools company, there was a distinct change in the attitude of the staff because they no longer took their jobs for granted. However, usually cultural change takes longer.

To achieve cultural change you will need to:

- destroy symbols of the old culture, for example throw out – or better still, publicly burn – the old manuals, close the management canteen, discontinue clocking in
- make a bold statement about the new culture and communicate this widely
- ensure that all of the management team understand, preach and live the new culture
- systematically remove from the organization those who are not prepared to embrace the new culture
- recruit using the requirements of the new culture and not compromise on this
- recognize and reward the new culture
- give incentives for adopting the new culture
- regularly monitor and assess the implementation of the new culture through observing behaviours and actions and gaining feedback from staff surveys.

There are many ways of doing this. Motorola's chief executive needed the organization to focus on quality and so he changed the board meeting agenda to discuss quality issues first. Then he left after the quality discussion, emphasizing again how important this was. Nevertheless, building a high-performing culture that extends throughout the organization is not easy.

Example: Disney

Probably one of the best examples of anchoring change is the Disney Corporation. In Florida, Disney employ 50,000 'cast members' (note the phrase, this is all about communicating the culture and values). The size is not the only problem. There is a high percentage of seasonal staff, staff turnover is relatively high and most cast members work well out of sight of their supervisor and in direct contact with the customer.

When Lee Cockerell, Executive Vice-President Operations, talked about managing such an operation, he used two words, 'educate' and 'enforce'. Management communicate the 'Disney Values' all the time. They measure the cast members' assessment of whether the managers live these values or not. They back this up with stories that capture what Disney is all about in the language of a theatrical performance: 'cast member', 'on stage', and so on. When things go wrong, managers personally intervene; senior managers will pick up paper in the park. But they also rely heavily on routines to ensure that the highest standards are met. Toilets, for example, are inspected regularly and repainted every two weeks.

These front-of-house performances are supported by highly sophisticated systems. Forecasts of attendance numbers run from five-year projections to 11 a.m. re-forecasts for the rest of that day. Cast members are then brought in or sent home based on this. Recruitment systems select on ability to perform. The job interview is much less important than how you perform in the test they present to you. If you are a chef, they get you to cook a meal; if you are a hotel manager, they visit your establishment to see for themselves and even interview your staff. Having ensured that they recruit only capable people, incentive schemes reward those who excel at their chosen profession. A top-performing waiter in a fine-dining restaurant can allegedly earn $60,000 a year, far more than the starting salary of a new manager.

Disney thinks that every job is important, no matter how menial it may appear to others. Every job has to be performed well for the organization to perform well, so they put effort into recruitment, management assessment and reward. This way they can communicate the culture right down to the very bottom of the organization and be sure that, in most circumstances, their people live their values.

Building a strong culture to the extent that Disney has achieved, and aligning their values, goals and levels of performance, is not easy. It is much easier to see and describe than replicate, but progress can be made given sufficient time, resources and commitment.

Managing people who will not change

There are nearly always people who will not accept change and it is important to manage these people – not to ignore them and leave them so that they become a continuing source of discontent. Eventually, those who will not accept change become the minority and become marginalized and many people leave of their own accord at this stage.

However, too much conflict is unproductive and, in the interests of having fully committed employees in your team, you will need to find a way to move those who do not leave and will not accept the change out of the organization. This might mean moving them to another part of the business or moving them out altogether. This gives out another signal that the change is here to stay. However you do this, make sure that you are being fair in arranging transfers or exits. Also, you will need to make the future attractive for those who are staying – their performance will drop if they fear 'death by a thousand cuts'.

● *Be as clear as possible about what will be different as a result of the change; watch what is actually happening (as opposed to what is being said) and make sure that actions are different in practice.*

● *When you have identified the signs that show that change has really happened, make sure that these signs are present throughout the business.*

● *Ensure that senior managers continue to act in a way that exemplifies what is needed following implementation of the changes.*

● *Never react too quickly – always give yourself thinking time.*

Summary

Embedding change is critical as without it all the time and effort will be wasted. Worse, the change will be seen to have failed and the organization will be at a disadvantage: either it will be uncompetitive in the market or be seen as failing in the eyes of the general public.

Structure and process are the easiest aspects to change as they will reinforce the new ways of working. Incentives and reward systems can help embed the change too, but cultural change is the most valuable to the organization. It is also the most elusive to achieve. To truly anchor change, you must change, at least in part, all three factors.

In tomorrow's chapter, we provide you with three tools to assess resistance to change. Understanding who is resisting the change, and why, is critical for successful change. At the planning stage it will give you the opportunity to manage the process, but keep coming back to these tools as resistance can easily trip you up in the transition, too.

SUNDAY MONDAY TUESDAY WEDNESDAY THURSDAY FRIDAY SATURDAY

Fact-check (answers at the back)

1. The refreezing stage is designed to ...
a) Freeze the change process ❏
b) Announce the end of the project ❏
c) Allow the project to be forgotten ❏
d) Stop the organization slipping back ❏

2. Calling the third phase refreezing is sometimes considered inappropriate as ...
a) Organisations often slip back ❏
b) Change should never be finished ❏
c) The phase is never reached ❏
d) Change should never be anchored ❏

3. Change should be anchored in ...
a) The company's structure ❏
b) The company's reward systems ❏
c) The company culture ❏
d) All of the above ❏

4. Appropriate performance measures can ...
a) Help anchor the change ❏
b) Confuse employees ❏
c) Be a substitute for good management ❏
d) Be all of these ❏

5. The key element in the reward system for anchoring a change is ...
a) The size of the reward ❏
b) The frequency with which it is paid out ❏
c) The alignment to the change ❏
d) The speed at which it is paid ❏

6. Organizational culture should come from ...
a) The example senior management set ❏
b) The shop floor ❏
c) The industry in which the company operates ❏
d) External consultants ❏

7. Which of the following is a symbol of the organization's culture?
a) The allocated parking places ❏
b) The dress code ❏
c) The lunchtime dining arrangements ❏
d) All of the above ❏

8. To change the organization's culture you need to ...
a) Pay well ❏
b) Continue recruitment in the same way ❏
c) Hold on to the past ❏
d) Remove those who don't want to change ❏

9. Structures and processes are ...
a) The hardest to change ❏
b) The easiest to change ❏
c) The last thing to change ❏
d) Irrelevant to change ❏

10. When managing the change process it is important to ...
a) React quickly ❏
b) Give yourself time to think ❏
c) Keep your distance ❏
d) Ignore resistance to the change ❏

Tools for analysing resistance to change

During Monday, Tuesday and Wednesday we looked at the three phases of change: unfreezing, moving and refreezing. Today we look closely at the tools for assessing the resistance to change.

'It is not necessary to change,' wrote the management guru W. Edward Deming. 'Survival is not mandatory.' However, most of us will know from our own experience that not everyone will agree with this sentiment, especially if they feel they may be adversely affected. As a manager implementing change, it sometimes feels as if some people are simply being obstructive towards anything new. As someone on the receiving end of change, you may feel that your organization is implementing far too many disruptive initiatives and wish to make your point heard.

One thing is certain. If you are implementing change, you will encounter resistance. For your change project to be successful, you will need to understand the key reasons for resistance and the forces for and against change. You will need to identify who the supporters are, who you need to influence and who the main objectors are. In this way, you can plan your tactics for overcoming resistance.

Why change is resisted

Ideally, potential resistance should be considered before the change project begins, but this chapter will help you to analyse what is happening as the change develops and to assess whether the change will stick.

Three different but complementary techniques are described today: force-field analysis, change responses, and priority, effort and reward assessment. But before we are introduced to these tools, it is useful to summarize some of the reasons why change is resisted:

- Lack of communication, so people do not:
  - understand what the change is
  - understand what the change means
  - understand why the change is necessary
  - see the urgency of the change
  - understand how the change fits into the bigger picture.
- Lack of will to change, because people do not:
  - want to change, they are comfortable the way they are
  - believe the change will deliver the expected benefits.

- Lack of acceptance of the change process, because people:
  - do not like the way the change is being handled
  - are not involved in the decision
  - are not consulted about the decision
  - do not like being told what to do
  - think they are being treated unfairly
  - think others are being treated unfairly.
- Lack of incentive to change because:
  - people do not see any personal advantage from the change
  - people do not see improvements in their working terms or conditions.
- Disadvantages of the new ways of working because the perception is that:
  - the job will become less interesting
  - the change will reduce their autonomy or work flexibility
  - the change will reduce social interaction
  - the change will break up the existing team.
- Threats of the change, because people see the change:
  - reducing their power
  - undermining their position and status
  - undermining their personal development
  - damaging their routes for promotion.

Bear these reasons in mind when using the tools described below.

Force-field analysis

One of the oldest and most frequently used techniques for analysing the resistance to change is force-field analysis. Force-field analysis is based on the premise that change will occur only if the forces driving the change are greater than the forces resisting the change.

Constructing a force-field analysis is a relatively easy exercise. You need to identify all of the forces driving the change and write them on the left-hand side of a sheet of paper, and then identify all of the forces blocking or resisting the change and write them on the other. Against each force, you should draw an arrow – the length of the arrow represents the strength of the force.

The result will be similar to Figure 5.1 below. The diagram can then be used to assess whether the change is likely to be successful or not, and to identify the greatest forces for change that have to be preserved and the forces resisting change that have to be undermined.

Advantages and shortcomings

The advantage of force-field analysis is its simplicity. It can be quickly used and the results easily communicated.

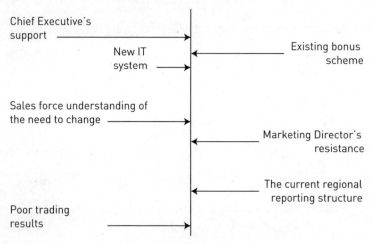

Figure 5.1 An example of a force-field analysis

However, force-field analysis does have shortcomings. First, it is very subjective and relies on an individual or a small group to identify all of the forces and make an informed assessment. Second, it assumes that projects occur in isolation whereas, in fact, most changes fail because they are simply overtaken by other changes or events, rather than stopped by lack of support or resistance.

Change responses

Professor Paul Strebel of the International Institute for Management Development suggests that resistance to change can be assessed by clustering those involved according to their response to the change. He suggests that there are two dimensions to be considered: the perceived potential impact (positive or negative) and the energy of the response (active or passive). The impact of change is often clear to see: a loss of position and power for some individuals, but an opportunity for advancement and new opportunities for others. However, the energy of response is less easy to identify because it depends on individuals' perceptions of the uncertainty of the change and their attitude to risk. The greater the risk and the more risk averse someone is, the more likely they are to be passive.

This approach creates four categories: traditionalists, bystanders, resistors and change agents (see Figure 5.2).

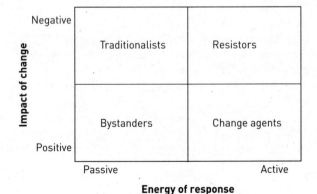

Figure 5.2 The four change categories

To identify the individuals who fall into the different groups, you need to ask four questions:

1 Who is likely to respond actively to the change and see it as an opportunity? (Change agents)
2 Who is likely to respond actively to the change and see it as a threat? (Resistors)
3 Who is likely to respond passively to the change and see it as an opportunity? (Bystanders)
4 Who is likely to respond passively to the change and see it as a threat? (Traditionalists)

Advantages and shortcomings

The advantage of using this tool is that it does categorize those involved in the change into four distinct camps and suggests a variety of incentives that can be applied to increase the level of commitment to the change. It can also be used quickly, to assess the position of those involved.

However, the technique does require some knowledge of those involved, especially to segregate the active from passive responders (although these differences will surface quickly once the change starts). It also assumes that you are dealing with a single major change project and so all the day-to-day interruptions do not influence the outcome.

Priority, effort and reward

This assessment tool is built on the theory that projects compete with each other for management time and attention. Therefore, whether a project will succeed or not will depend on the effort available, the expected benefits the project is likely to bring and the consequent priority the project receives. This was shown to be the case in a study of 88 change projects spread across six different UK manufacturing businesses between 1998 and 2000 and the tool described is very effective in establishing whether or not a project is likely to succeed.

Using the tool

In its simplest form, the tool can be used by individually interviewing each of the managers and key actors who are to be directly involved in the change project. They should be asked:

- What are the major improvement projects that will occupy your time and effort over the next three to six months?
- Please rank these projects in their order of importance, as you currently perceive it, by allocating 100 points between all of the improvement projects.
- If you were given 100 points of your effort to split between these projects, how much of your effort would each project take to make reasonable progress over the next three to six months?
- If the projects take 100 points of effort, how much of your effort is required just to complete the day-to-day routine task of your job?
- If the total points of effort for the projects and routine activities is, say, 200, then what in your opinion is your total available effort?

This approach will allow you to:

- identify all of the projects currently competing for management time and effort
- produce an approximate priority ranking of the current projects
- identify the level of support that the new change project is receiving (from its relative position in the ranking)
- assess whether those involved are, or expect to be, overloaded by their day-to-day work or volume of improvement projects.

An example

It is useful to create a picture of the situation, by drawing up a table in the form of Figure 5.3. Figure 5.3 has been created from the data gathered through the interview and is illustrated in Figure 5.4.

This figure shows that the cultural change project currently has the highest priority, but that the Managing Director is not going to spend a great deal of effort on it. It also shows that, after taking into account the day-to-day demands of the job, the Managing Director considers that he is overloaded.

Project rank	Improvement project descriptions	Effort required
50	Cultural change project	30
30	Cost reduction exercise	50
20	New market identification	20
1 Total improvement project effort required		100
2 Total effort required for everyday job		100
3 Total effort required (1+2)		200
4 Total effort available (individual's assessment)		180

Figure 5.3 Interview responses from Managing Director

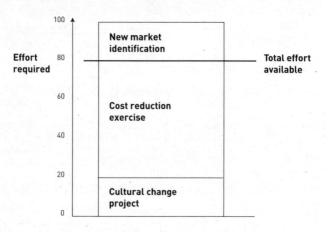

Figure 5.4 Graphical representation of the Managing Director's improvement projects

There should be concerns about whether the new market identification project is going to be completed or progress will go to schedule.

Advantages and shortcomings

The advantage of using this tool is that it provides a way of assessing the potential success and failure of projects by engaging with those who expect to be directly involved. It provides feedback in the form of priorities, and identifies potential areas of concern.

The technique has one final major benefit: it does not directly ask whether the person being interviewed supports the project or not. It is much easier for managers to argue that other projects should have higher priority and, therefore, show their resistance to a project by the position it is placed on the graph – often the lowest priority.

This approach has the shortcoming of requiring the nature of the project to be disclosed before the assessment can be made. Sometimes issues of confidentiality prevent this from happening.

TIPS

- *Never do the analysis of resistance to change on your own. You have only one point of view and involving others will be invaluable.*

- *Start the process of persuasion early, especially with the most important resistors. It will take time.*

- *In many organizations there are several big initiatives running concurrently. People can feel that their effort is being dissipated in different directions. They may also feel these initiatives are not helping them meet their own goals.*

- *The trick is to link the projects together so that people can see the big picture and understand that the initiatives are all pieces of the same jigsaw – they are connected and are needed to create the whole.*

- *At the start, you will often find some important people are quite sceptical or opposed to the change. If you can make them supporters, you will give the change a great boost, especially if you can use them later to help with the implementation.*

- *In a major change, some important individuals will always be opposed. Be prepared to sacrifice them or the change; you can rarely have both.*

- *How you treat resistors is important for the change process. The way they are handled legitimizes the change to those who are left. Always go the extra mile to try to convince resistors, but then act as humanely as you can in finding other roles or terminating their employment contracts.*

Summary

Today we reviewed three specific tools for analysing change:

- *Force-field analysis:* you should use this as a quick tool to assess subjectively the largest forces driving and impeding your change initiative.
  - *Change responses:* you should use this to categorize people into groups – your allies, your enemies and those simply sitting on the fence.
- *Priority, effort and reward assessment:* you should use this both to understand the stresses on the organization and to identify where you have support or problems.

Before a major change, always conduct an analysis or assessment. You can't plan a change properly without understanding the issues and where people stand, so use the tools at your disposal. Don't forget the tools are also useful for analysing why an initiative has stalled, so you should use them at all stages of a change project.

Tomorrow we consider three real change projects in detail, drawing out the aspects we have covered so far.

Fact-check (answers at the back)

1. In a large project, change ...
   a) Is never resisted ❑
   b) Always has some people who will resist ❑
   c) Is always resisted by everyone ❑
   d) Is never to anyone's benefit ❑

2. Change is resisted because ...
   a) People don't feel consulted ❑
   b) People don't like the way it is handled ❑
   c) They think they are unfairly treated ❑
   d) Of all of the above ❑

3. For individuals, the rationale for resisting the change is that ...
   a) They lose position and status ❑
   b) They lose power ❑
   c) Promotion routes are blocked ❑
   d) All of the above are true ❑

4. The shortcomings of force-field analysis are ...
   a) It is very subjective ❑
   b) It assumes resistance is the only reason why change fails ❑
   c) It focuses on only one project ❑
   d) All of the above ❑

5. The change response tool focuses on ...
   a) Different change projects ❑
   b) Junior staff ❑
   c) Top management ❑
   d) Categorizing individuals into groups ❑

6. The shortcomings of the change response tool are ...
   a) It is very subjective ❑
   b) It assumes resistance is the only reason why change fails ❑
   c) It focuses on only one project ❑
   d) All of the above ❑

7. The major advantage of the priority, effort and reward tool is ...
   a) It is simple to use ❑
   b) It is the only approach ❑
   c) It is subjective ❑
   d) People don't have to say yes or no to supporting the project ❑

8. The major blind spot of the priority, effort and reward tool is ...
   a) It focuses only on resistance to change ❑
   b) It ignores other projects ❑
   c) It misses parent organization initiatives ❑
   d) It is subjective ❑

9. You should use the tools to analyse resistance to change ...
   a) At the beginning of the project ❑
   b) As the project progresses ❑
   c) If the change starts to stall ❑
   d) At all of the above stages ❑

10. For change to succeed you must be prepared to ...
    a) Compromise your principles ❑
    b) Act in an underhand way ❑
    c) Sacrifice people ❑
    d) Do all of the above ❑

FRIDAY

Examples of change projects

So far we have looked at individual aspects and stages of a change management project. We have looked at why change is necessary and at creating the impetus for change. We have looked at how you implement the change and at the various ways in which people will react. We have looked at how you make change stick and become part of normal working practice and we have provided you with some tools for analysing the resistance to change that you will, inevitably, meet.

However, a change management project does not follow an orderly, linear course. Each project is different, with its own set of problems. You need to be flexible in your approach while acting in a consistent manner and remaining faithful to your original objectives. If you take too rigid a stance, you will store up problems; if you do not remain true to your stated objectives, people will not take you seriously and your position will be undermined. You need to apply different tools in different circumstances and carefully assess what is happening and how you need to adapt your approach.

Today you will be given three very different examples of change projects. Each case is based on real change initiatives but they are all fictitious as they combine experiences from different settings to create authentic but publishable examples.

THE THEORY   THE PRACTICE

Building a customer-focused team

This study is based on a real service organization, which was long established and had been highly successful with little real competition. It had not changed for many years but was feeling the effects of new competition and declining revenues.

The situation

- Staff had been recruited for their organizational and administrative skills and not for their ability to handle customers.
- Systems were set up for the ease of the staff, rather than for the customer.
- The structure was hierarchical: each person had a rigid job description and a supervisor to ensure that things were done properly; generally work was carried out to a high standard.
- Everyone arrived promptly at 9 a.m. and finished promptly at 5 p.m. with an hour for lunch between 1 p.m. and 2 p.m.
- The organization had a paternalistic approach, almost cocooning the staff from commercial realities; while this

created a very loyal staff team and minimized staff turnover, it led to complacency and a lack of new ideas that would normally come in through the arrival of new staff.

The need for change

Revenues had been declining in real terms over a number of years, but had been offset by cost-cutting to maintain a reasonable 'bottom line'. This might have continued, yet the senior management team faced a particularly challenging year when further cost-cutting became just too painful. It became evident that customers were 'voting with their feet' because the organization was not providing the service they wanted.

It was decided that, if changes were not made, the organization would not survive. In particular, there was an urgent need to find out why customers were leaving and what they were really looking for and, as a result, to adjust the services in the company's portfolio. There was also a need to focus the staff on commercial realities and the importance of customer service.

Changes required

As a result of customer research, the senior management team identified several areas for major change. One of the largest of these was the need to create a change in the culture of the organization. Without this underlying change, it would be impossible to introduce new services and to beat the competition. Major requirements of the change were to:

- focus staff on the commercial reality – revenue as well as cost – and on providing customer service (as well as administrative excellence)
- create flexibility in the staff team, rather than have rigid job descriptions, to ensure that customers' enquiries could be handled much faster and that future ongoing changes could be handled smoothly
- remove layers of supervision to take out some staff costs and to avoid duplication of work.

This necessitated the following specific changes:

- Restructuring the department to redeploy supervisors in roles that involved adding value, rather than simply checking
- Negotiating flexible working hours to keep the customer enquiry line open from 8.30 a.m. until 5.30 p.m.
- Rewriting job descriptions
- Training staff in new skills
- Changing the culture to one where staff used their own initiative, rather than waiting for direction, and where customers were recognized as being important.

All this had to be done in a way that would retain the values of the organization (especially the values relating to high-quality work and the maintenance of staff loyalty).

The solution

A departmental meeting was held to explain the company's position and to discuss what this meant for the department. The problem of declining sales and the drop in customer numbers was highlighted, and ideas for change were floated – some presented as 'must happen' and others as 'how can we achieve this?'

Some useful ideas came out of this discussion, but many individuals thought that this was purely a 'management' problem and felt that they had nothing to contribute. There was also a feeling that the proposed changes would add too much work to a workload perceived as being too heavy already. The supervisors felt strongly that work standards would decline dramatically if supervision was taken away and this would result in the loss of even more customers.

From this meeting it became apparent that the team had little experience of some of the realities of the commercial world in which they were operating. Benchmarking visits to teams with similar functions were arranged in non-competing local organizations. Groups within the team were asked to plan for these visits in advance, drawing attention to the issues that they wanted to raise at the visits and to the observations that they should make. After the visits there was discussion about what had been learned and what could be implemented. This had several effects including:

- Team members began to realize that they had good ideas which could contribute to the discussion of the organization's future.
- They realized that flexible working was the norm, and that their situation was rather better than some individuals working in call centres, where work was very closely monitored indeed.
- They began to see how other companies handled their customers.
- They became dissatisfied with the current way of working, feeling that they could, after all, improve on what they were doing.

Following these visits, supervisors were asked to consider ways in which they could add value and improve customer service, using what they had seen in other organizations. This helped to provide a focus on what they were *moving to* in their new roles (and gave them a say in defining those roles) rather than thinking all the time about what they were *moving from*.

Formal training was carried out in key areas, such as customer service, but also in some of the 'softer' skills, including personal effectiveness, decision making and time management. This helped to boost confidence and provided the feeling that the company was investing in its people.

Job roles were reviewed and redrawn with the promise that they would be reappraised at frequent periods and changes made as necessary. The new roles were also discussed with every individual, to provide a 'feel' for the overall objective of that role and how it contributed to the overall success of the company. Expectations of how that role would work were also discussed, including the expectation that the individuals would work as much as possible on their own initiative and would have the freedom (within certain limitations) to take whatever action was necessary to please the customer.

Standards of performance were set and agreed, including measures of customer service.

The outcome

The first few weeks of working were difficult. Staff continually went to their ex-supervisors for guidance, which the supervisors gladly gave. There were rumblings that the performance measures (which they had agreed were achievable) were, in fact, totally unrealistic. They found it tiring and difficult to deal with customers. They were unclear what the limits of their responsibility were and they missed the structure of the old regime. In fact, there was a great deal of dissatisfaction.

This was the point where the management team had to stick to their guns. The ex-supervisors were coached to ask further questions, so that staff could make their own decisions, rather than be given easy solutions. Over time, supervisors realized that they had a more important role to fill and would not have time to deal with staff queries all day. Performance measures were maintained and represented pictorially to provide a visual measure of progress. Improvement towards meeting these targets was rewarded and praised. Some members of the team were encouraged to go out and meet customers with the sales team so that they could see their problems first hand.

It took several months – and some disagreement between members of the team – before the new ways of working became the norm. Nevertheless, gradually this did happen. Staff became very keen to meet their performance targets; they relished the idea of going out to see customers and, in doing so, brought back new ideas for improving service. The 9 a.m.–5 p.m. mentality disappeared as staff became really involved in their work. Above all, sales began to improve.

Western Engineering

Background

Western Engineering was a company with a long history going back over 250 years. The main manufacturing site employed over 500 people and produced a wide range of consumable products used in applications as diverse as medical devices, nuclear power plants and petrochemical plants. These products were sold across the world to original equipment manufacturers and the maintenance market.

The manufacturing site had been run for many years as a single business unit, managed by a dictatorial managing director. His style had been to drive high levels of performance through personally, ensuring that the staff did what they were told. However, as he neared retirement, the business performance had started to tail off. His successor was a much younger man and came not only from outside the company, but from outside the industry.

The problem

Once installed in his new position, the Managing Director set about improving the fortunes of the business. He knew that profitability could be better than it was and that customer service was far from the level desired. The company had been trading for several years on its long reputation, but now new and cheaper products were coming into the market, many from the Far East.

To increase responsibility and customer focus, he reorganized the business into three separate business units, each responsible for manufacturing and selling distinct parts of the product range. However, because of the size of the site, he could not afford to have each business unit self-contained, so there were a number of services shared by the business units: accounting, IT and distribution.

The Managing Director also wrote a new business plan, setting out the new direction for the business. After 12 months it was becoming clear that the changes were not working. In particular:

- The new management team did not understand the business plan. They had not bought into it and they were still waiting for the new Managing Director to tell them what they had to do, in the way that they had been told in the past.
- The service functions continued as a law unto themselves. They were headed by individuals who had been very senior managers under the old structure and, therefore, ignored requests for changes in service from the three new business units.

- To try to overcome some of these difficulties, the Managing Director had brought in consultants to implement a new performance measurement system and this had been spectacularly unsuccessful.

The Managing Director fervently believed that what he was proposing was right for the business, but the history and culture of the company were preventing his vision from being properly implemented. He was also starting to be concerned about his position and credibility, being new to both the industry and the company.

The solution

The solution to the problem was in itself quite simple – to involve the whole management team in the development of a new strategy and in the implementation of a new performance measurement system. This was achieved through a series of workshops over a three-month period, and created the vehicle to implement the changes required.

The series of facilitated workshops used particular tools to analyse the business, set objectives and design appropriate performance measures. The whole management team was involved. They started by assessing their customers' wants and needs, and segmenting the customer base. Having established this, they went on to consider what the company was trying to achieve and the requirements of the other stakeholders, including the owners, managers and employees.

The process was not easy and there was a great deal of argument and debate, but it was agreed at the beginning that this facilitated, inclusive approach was to be taken. The only time the project nearly came off the rails was when the Managing Director decided that the team were proposing too many new performance measures and intervened to drastically reduce the number to a number of his own choosing. This did not go down well with the Business Unit General Managers who felt that the process was being usurped, and they colluded together over the next series of workshops and reintroduced a significant number of key performance indicators.

Resistance

Despite the workshops, there was still resistance to the change within the service functions. The new structure required them to provide services to the new business units and some of the managers believed that, because of their previous positions, they had the right to provide the service they wanted to and not what their internal customer required. In one function, this reached the stage of the manager explicitly resisting the implementation of the new performance measures and actively engaging in undermining the process.

The individual involved was a senior, long-serving and well-respected individual. He undoubtedly possessed great technical skills and his actions were blocking the progress of the project. For a time, the new Managing Director was undecided as to the course of action. The new strategy and measures needed to be implemented, and the service functions needed to focus on supporting the new business units, but this was being thwarted by a senior manager. The Managing Director tried persuasion and reason on numerous occasions, but this failed and so he had no alternative but to terminate the individual's contract of employment.

The outcome

The results of the process were very clear to see. For the first time, the senior management team of the company had a strategy they all understood, that they had all been involved in creating. They also had a clear understanding of their objectives and targets, which had been incorporated in the performance measures they had designed. These measures then communicated the direction to the rest of the business and were enthusiastically implemented by the managers.

The managers' behaviour also changed. Instead of asking what they should be doing, they now knew what was required – they had to improve the performance of the company on the measures that had been accepted. Over a short period of time, managers moved from doing as they were told to taking their own initiatives, and decision-making authority was cascaded down the organization. Customer service improved and profitability rapidly followed.

Why did the change work?

So often in change management it is not the change itself that does not work, it is the way it is undertaken that prevents the change occurring. The process adopted here had the effect of:

- ensuring the involvement and participation of the whole senior management team
- explaining to the team what the company needed to achieve and why
- creating a shared understanding of the strategy
- developing buy-in to the measures, and a commitment to implement them.

Finally, the termination of the employment contract of the senior manager resisting the new approach showed all concerned how far the company was prepared to go to get the project implemented.

Maintenance Services

Background

Maintenance Services was the UK business of an international group. The company had successfully operated for many years, but the company's competitive position had been declining, together with falling levels of profitability. At the annual wage round, the union asked for an across-the-board, above-inflation increase. However, the economic climate made this unaffordable.

To move forward, the company had to increase its productivity and this meant greater flexibility from the workforce. When these needs were discussed with the union, their response was that the company was rich enough to afford the claim. In fact, the company had always paid claims in the past, even at the height of the recession, when demand had drastically fallen. The union was not prepared to listen to a presentation on the company's financial position. They preferred to stick to their claim and to ignore the management's requests to negotiate more flexible ways of working.

Building the burning platform

The management were concerned about the situation, but there was no compelling case to do something different. An outside, interim HR director was brought in to assess the situation and after a few days she summarized the position in a series of seven statements, as follows:

1 The company's competitive position and profitability are declining.
2 Deregulation in the industry will mean that, in future, competition will become even more intense.
3 The major source of cost disadvantage is labour costs.
4 Just conceding to the current wage claim, without any improvements in flexibility, would make this situation worse.
5 In the past, the company has always conceded to wage demands.
6 Because of the competitive situation, this year's demand cannot be accepted.
7 If the company does not confront the labour productivity problem this year, it will be in a much weaker position to do so next year.

This simple set of statements encapsulated the company's position. It created the initial burning platform needed to confront the issue, and galvanized the management to action. But the company was not prepared for a strike – it needed time. The procedure agreed with the union for settling disputes provided some of this time, and UK industrial relations legal requirements for notice and ballots provided the rest.

First steps

The first step was to request arbitration through ACAS (Advisory, Conciliation and Arbitration Service). Preparation for the meeting took a couple of weeks and the union had to listen to the company's presentation of its financial position.

However, this attempt at reconciliation did not work; the union still pressed their claim regardless of the management's position – but the process bought time.

Shortly after the meeting, the union issued notice of a ballot for industrial action.

The company's response

In response to the notice of the ballot, the company took two approaches: first, to communicate with the workforce to achieve a 'no' vote and, second, to prepare for a strike.

The communication campaign was more than the company had ever done before. Besides notes in pay packets, letters were sent to all home addresses designed to arrive on Saturday morning. Three waves of face-to-face communications were planned and because of the 24-hour nature of the operation, managers were trained to deliver these quickly to all the shifts in one cycle. The process of preparing, honing and delivering these communications involved one-third of the management team.

The preparations for a strike were also extensive. A PR firm was engaged to help handle the press, lawyers were commissioned to advise on industrial relations and employment law, and a security firm was hired to protect against sabotage. A call for volunteers was sent out for management support, and an agency contracted to recruit a replacement workforce. Customers were informed and contingency plans put in place to simplify menus and to cater certain flights from overseas.

While all of this preparation was happening, the senior management team was assessing the consequences of a strike. Apart from the disruption, consideration was also given to the changes in working practices that the company might be able to introduce if a significant section of the workforce were dismissed during the strike. These were substantial. Therefore, a plan emerged that focused on dealing with any industrial action quickly and decisively, to minimize the impact on the business and to move the company to a new way of working.

The ballot result

Despite the huge communication campaign, there was a 3–1 vote in favour of the strike. All of the company's work was undermined in a single mass meeting, when the works convener simply got up and said 'Forget what management is saying; if you back us we will get you more.'

The ballot result was communicated, together with seven days' notice of the first of two one-day strikes. The company immediately responded by rescheduling all of the shift rotas so that all employees were scheduled to work on the day of the strike. Letters were issued to all employees, informing them of the new schedules and warning them that non-attendance would be considered strike action and that all strikers would be dismissed. When the union received this message, they were expecting a request for further negotiations, and they were shocked.

Another mass meeting was called because many wanted to know whether the management's threat was legal. When the answer was 'yes', the mood changed. Many of the employees were earning very good money and did not want to lose their jobs. The union requested a further meeting, which was accepted after they agreed to rescind the strike threat. Within hours a deal was agreed and the crisis was over.

Why the change?

On reflection, it was not what the management *said* that made the difference – the union had heard the management's rhetoric for years before – it was what was *done*. The staff had seen the preparations. They had received the communications, the letters and the notes in the payslips.

They also noted that the responses were pre-planned – the communications were received too quickly to have been otherwise. They had seen the crisis centre being set up, the visits from the security advisers. The relief managers had started to arrive and staff knew that customers were being informed. They also knew that agency staff were being recruited and trained. But, alongside all of this, there was a change in management attitude; they had a purpose and went round whistling 'There is going to be trouble in the morning'.

The incident totally changed the industrial relations climate in the business. Staff were not paid any less and there were no redundancies, but they realized that they had to work for their money, not just be paid for attendance. Many of the expensive practices that paid staff just for being at work were discontinued. Productivity issues could now be discussed and improvements agreed. Performance improved and profitability followed.

Comment

Mature businesses are the products of their own history.

Sometimes old structures and practices hold the business back and sometimes they can even destroy it. Making big changes in these circumstances is seen as either impossible or too dangerous to contemplate; nevertheless, as this case shows, it can be done. To make these big changes requires considerable commitment. To succeed, you need:

- **a compelling case for change** – the seven statements provided this because they woke the company up to its long-term declining position
- **a vision of the future** – this came from the realization of how competitive the business could be if the current practices could be abolished
- **a means of achieving the vision** – this emerged through the contingency planning and preparations for the strike.

Management commitment was truly developed as the crisis evolved. The small senior team increasingly involved the rest of the management, first in the communications and then in the planning. From a small group, the team grew to include the whole management team and that created a momentum of its own. Ownership of the problem was spread more widely, giving the team a purpose. That is how the real change happened.

Summary

Every change project is different, in size, in complexity and in impact. Therefore, each change should be managed differently. Don't fall into the trap of simply taking the approach that worked when you used it last time. You may be lucky and it may work again. But if you haven't properly analysed the situation, you could either be using a sledgehammer to crack a nut or come unstuck on something you missed. Change is hard enough without you making it harder by not adapting your approach to the situation in hand.

However, all change goes through the phases of preparation ('unfreezing'), the real change ('moving') and embedding the new way of working ('refreezing'). Learn to listen for the different phase of your change. Are people still arguing about the need and purpose of the change? If so, you are still unfreezing. Or are they talking about the mechanics and wrestling with problems? If so, you are moving. Or have they gone quiet? If so, you are either embedding, or unravelling, so be especially careful here.

Tomorrow we will summarize and provide guidance on the management behaviours, roles and responsibilities required to make the change happen.

SUNDAY MONDAY TUESDAY WEDNESDAY THURSDAY FRIDAY SATURDAY

Fact-check (answers at the back)

1. To get people to deliver high performance it is best to ...
   a) Focus on their KPIs ❏
   b) Focus on their job description ❏
   c) Focus on the customer ❏
   d) Focus on doing what their boss requires ❏

2. Benchmarking can be helpful as it ...
   a) Shows real examples of different approaches ❏
   b) Opens people's eyes ❏
   c) Is a good source of new ideas ❏
   d) Does all of the above ❏

3. Staff work best when they ...
   a) Have a complete task to do ❏
   b) Have a very tightly defined activity ❏
   c) Have limited responsibilities ❏
   d) Have supervisors to solve all their problems ❏

4. A business plan is ...
   a) Not effective ❏
   b) Always effective ❏
   c) Only effective when it is widely understood ❏
   d) Only useful for the CEO ❏

5. Facilitated strategy workshops ...
   a) Help engage the senior team ❏
   b) Often change the direction of the organization ❏
   c) Create understanding ❏
   d) Do all of the above ❏

6. During a facilitated strategy workshop you should ...
   a) Contribute only when asked ❏
   b) Have the right to say what you want ❏
   c) Toe the company line ❏
   d) Defer to the opinion of your seniors ❏

7. After decisions have been made in a facilitated strategy workshop, you should ...
   a) Contribute only when asked ❏
   b) Have the right to say what you want ❏
   c) Toe the company line ❏
   d) Carry on as before ❏

8. A position statement designed to create the need for change should include ...
   a) Something about competitive pressures ❏
   b) Reasons for acting now ❏
   c) A clear rationale for change ❏
   d) All of the above ❏

9. Rhetoric is ...
   a) Always believed ❏
   b) Never believed ❏
   c) More likely to be believed when aligned to action ❏
   d) A waste of time ❏

10. Management commitment to large-scale change
    a) Will be strongly tested ❏
    b) Will be assumed ❏
    c) Is never an issue ❏
    d) Is never the reason for a change to fail ❏

SATURDAY

Making change happen

Organizations comprise people who all have their own opinions, which they express to a greater or lesser extent. It is not even as simple as that. We all know that what people say is not necessarily what they really mean. Understanding behaviour is an important part of managing the change process. Once you understand what is really happening, who is causing problems, and why, you have a better chance of tackling those problems and reaching a successful outcome.

It is essential to deal with resistors to change, difficult though that is. Many managers try to avoid it and ignore what is happening in front of their eyes. If you do not deal with resistors, you will make your project harder to implement successfully and may leave behind the seeds of its undoing in the future. But it is important that you do not spend all your time overcoming objections. You also need to gain commitment. You need to get people involved and give them a role.

In today's chapter we will look at the all-important senior management commitment to change, at the allocation of roles and responsibilities and at practical ways in which you can create the best environment for your project to succeed.

Senior management commitment to change

As with any major initiative, top management commitment is essential for a successful outcome. In fact, there is more to it than just 'commitment'. At a time of change, employees are naturally more sensitive to senior management behaviour, and actions and words are subject to more scrutiny and interpretation than usual.

The prevailing attitudes can usually be described as follows:

- Lack of trust
- People looking for reasons to avoid the changes completely, or to tone them down (and this can be among those implementing changes as well as among those subjected to them)
- Vociferous individuals searching for, and articulating, reasons why the changes will not work
- An inward-looking focus, concentrating on what is happening within the organization rather than watching what is happening to the business as a whole.

So, how can senior managers handle this?

1 **The senior management team needs to share a clear picture of what is to be achieved by change and a structure for achieving these aims.**

The team should plan what change is required and why, whether this is to be a major shake-up or an ongoing process, and produce a schedule of activities with a timescale. Within this plan there are likely to be some aims, activities and timescales that will be sacrosanct. If these are not met, then the change process will fail. They act as pillars around which everything else must be built. Everyone in the senior team needs to know what these are and to keep them in mind throughout the change process.

Having established the plan and the 'immovable pillars', it is critical that senior managers stick to them. When obstacles appear, it is tempting to take an easier course and change the plan. While this may be necessary in some cases (no plan can account for every eventuality), if the 'immovable pillars' are changed, then the whole course of the change process may be derailed. These 'immovable pillars' can be used as a benchmark for testing whether an action is in line with the overall aims. An 'immovable pillar' within a change, designed to improve customer service, might, for example, be to develop an account management system where there is a single point of contact for particular customers within the organization. This may entail major restructuring and retraining of staff, but may also be essential to the future well-being of the business. If a department then sets out a well-argued case for two points of contact (say, service and new sales), this proposal can be measured against the overarching aim (and rejected).

2 **Messages given out by the senior team must be consistent.**

If one manager says one thing and another something else, then integrity is compromised. The lack of agreement can be used to 'divide and conquer' or to cast doubt on management's ability to handle the process.

3 Everyone involved in the process must pay attention to detail.

In the overwhelming amount of planning and activity that is involved in major change projects, details can easily be overlooked. The process must be thought through step by step at a fairly early stage, using 'What if?' questions. To use the account management scenario, one might analyse all types of existing customer queries to identify exactly how these would be handled by one point of contact. What if we have a query about…? Or…?

This achieves two things:

a It uncovers any latent problems in the original proposals

b When the inevitable 'We can't do this because…' arises, senior managers have an answer and are able to show that they have thought through the detail. (Having said this, senior managers are often 'big picture' people and, by the nature of their job, are further removed from day-to-day detail.) Another approach is to create a working group of people who are involved in the everyday working and ask them to come up with solutions.

4 There must be excellent communication within the senior management team.

Good communication plays an important part in making sure that the management team present a strong and united front. In a real case study, several key managers involved in fashioning and implementing a major restructuring project were forced to reach a compromise with various groups on original proposals, for political expediency. Records of these compromises had not been kept in one place, nor widely communicated, and came to light only during the implementation process when the groups involved produced documents exempting them from part of the changes. This damaged implementation and reduced the benefits achieved.

5 Information should come through the senior management team and not through the grapevine.

The senior management team should be as open as possible about what is happening, setting out the whole picture and creating opportunities for open dialogue. Giving out information in an uncontrolled way can be risky because it allows the grapevine to work and to distort facts.

How senior management act and behave during a major change programme is crucial. Those opposing the change will be looking for the slightest chink in the management's armour, an indication that someone is not whole-heartedly in favour, any lever which they can turn to their advantage. Keeping senior management 'on message' is, therefore, an essential task.

On stage – backstage

What we have just described is top management's public commitment to change. This is the equivalent of a theatrical performance 'on stage', in front of the audience. In any theatrical performance, the audience does not see what is happening backstage, but the backstage activity is necessary for the play to be performed. The same is true of any major change. The trick is to keep the backstage activities out of sight so they do not distract the audience from the performance on stage.

Backstage activities will include:

- **Negotiations between the key players** as to the direction and scope of the change – an initial consensus will be required and this usually requires some hard bargaining between very senior players, but this should be well out of sight of most employees
- **Conflicts between the senior executives** over the vision, strategy or mechanics of the change – with a strong management team this is highly probable. Individuals will have strong views and express them forcefully. If this conflict is handled constructively, a better solution can emerge, but this activity needs to be done behind closed doors. A private argument followed by a public display of unity on a chosen strategy is worth its weight in gold
- **Anxiety of the sponsor** about whether the change will be successful – this is common: any good leader should have concerns, and sharing them with close colleagues will help bind the team as well as helping the development of plans

and actions. But in most organizations these anxieties cannot be discussed in public. Most organizations want strong direction.

So, when managing change it is important for everybody involved to know when they are 'on stage' and when they are 'off stage' – when they can disagree and argue and when they have to toe the party line. In business, the stage area is not always as obvious to see as it is in a theatre. A better analogy is probably the Disney cast member – as soon as he or she puts on their costume, they are on stage and have to remain in character until they return to the dressing room. Senior executives and change team members should follow the same example. Those who deliberately pull up the curtain to reveal backstage turmoil for their own advantage need to be dealt with severely.

You will need to find a way of defining what is on stage and backstage. Some suggestions might be:

- Change steering committee meetings are backstage – everything else is on stage.
- Strategy content meetings are backstage – implementation meetings are on stage.
- Backstage activity is allowed until we make a decision – after the decision we are all on stage toeing the agreed company line.

Roles and responsibilities

Management commitment to change is essential, but responsibility for the change will have to be delegated. Others will have to take ownership of the change and it is important that the handover processes are handled smoothly. Clear definitions of roles and responsibilities will make this happen.

In a large change, different people will manage each of the different roles. If you are managing a small change, the roles are still important but the same person might fill multiple roles.

The sponsor

This is the senior executive who has the power and authority to initiate the change. In a large-scale change, the sponsor will often be the Chief Executive. In a smaller change, it may be the head of department or function in which the change is taking place.

The sponsor's role is to initiate and guide the change, but they usually do not undertake the change themselves. This role may include:

- chairing the change steering committee
- choosing the various teams involved
- appointing the change manager
- ensuring that the project is properly resourced
- communicating the purpose and commitment to change
- reviewing progress
- celebrating successes
- removing roadblocks.

It is very tempting for the sponsor to take on the role of change manager as well. This should be avoided. The sponsor may well feel that by championing the change they will have greater control over implementation, but this excludes others and the transfer of ownership is lost. Even for a relatively small change, it is useful for the sponsor to find someone else to be the change agent. When this happens, at least there are now two of you against the rest of the world.

The steering committee

The steering committee should comprise the senior executives directly affected by the decisions being taken and the changes being made. They will need to discuss the strategy and implications and agree to the changes proceeding. Specialists, strategic planners and others may augment this team with special skills to make the change happen. Usually, the change agent will also join this team at the appropriate stage in the project.

The role of the steering committee will include:

- discussing the situation, proposed actions and general direction of the change
- agreeing the actions planned
- supporting the change through communication to the rest of the organization
- reporting back concerns and potential barriers to the change
- supporting the sponsor in their deliberations and decisions.

Again, in small changes it is tempting to dispense with this group. But even if you only get a small group of key people together informally, at particular points in the process, you will discover the benefit of having a team behind the change. Involving people in the change creates commitment as it strengthens the sense of ownership. This makes success more likely.

It is useful to make the steering committee porous, that is to say, allowing people to join and leave the group quite freely. Doing this will stop 'groupthink' – everyone agreeing to an action because they have not fully considered all the alternatives. It will stop the committee becoming too bureaucratic and the composition of skills required will alter as the project progresses. It is also important to ensure that the group does not get too removed from everybody else in the organization.

The change manager

The change manager is the person who will take day-to-day responsibility for the management of the change project. They may work alone or lead a team, but they will require the support of the steering committee to complete their task.

The choice of change manager is critical. He or she must have the time to dedicate to the project and in larger projects this will require relinquishing their usual responsibilities. Often, this rules out very senior executives, but the change manager still has to have credibility and command respect from the rest of the organization. He or she must also be trusted, and a reputation for being an 'honest broker' is a great advantage.

This role will usually include:

- managing the project resources on a day-to-day basis
- supporting the steering committee in its deliberations
- communicating all aspects of the change
- managing the detail of the change
- reporting back to the steering committee perceptions of the change from the rest of the organization
- reporting back progress and obstacles.

The implementation team

The steering committee needs to be involved in the implementation, but the size of the task will usually require a separate implementation team. This should be the line managers of those areas being changed. Involving the line managers ensures that the change becomes embedded and is another method of rolling out the change.

The role of the implementation team will usually include:

- communicating the change
- training those involved in the new ways of working
- managing the transition
- feeding back progress.

It is useful to create the implementation team quite early in the process so that they are at least aware of, if not partially involved, in the change debate. The more they are involved, the greater their ownership and commitment. Using the line mangers to communicate the change and train those involved is a powerful lever to use in implementation. To train others, the team will have to be fully conversant with the change and this is important for a successful implementation.

Try to use line managers rather than staff teams. A staff team will lack credibility and undermine the position of the line managers, so staff teams are best avoided.

Other roles

There may be other roles that occur in specific situations, for example, co-ordination is a particular problem in bigger organizations. There may also be a debate about using external consultants, but if you do this remember to take control. The consultants will be gone one day and you will be left to manage what they have done.

Even in small changes, think about:

- initiating the change – the power and authority required
- directing the change – getting the right input and making the right decisions
- managing the change – the resources, details and co-ordination
- implementing the change – line managers and supervisors making it happen.

Effective change

Many organizations have a long list of change initiatives they are trying to implement. In these organizations, surviving change management initiatives becomes a competence. As a result, the organization does not improve.

Reducing the number of change initiatives is one way of overcoming this problem. Prioritize and focus! But there is another way of consolidating past change management projects: do not allow projects to have an end. If you do, the project is finished, the attention moves to the next one and the benefits may be quickly lost. A much better way is to roll the projects together – make the next project an extension of the last and build on it, rather than destroy it (see Figure 7.1).

For example, if you had a big push on developing the strategy last year and this year you want to implement a new performance measurement system, then link the two. Make the performance measurement project a means of deploying the strategy – this way you will build on last year's project rather than losing it. Similarly, if you have now implemented the performance measurement system and you need to develop the way annual appraisals are done, ensure that the work in Human Resources builds on the objectives and measures you have already developed. Too often, previous initiatives are forgotten and are buried under the next.

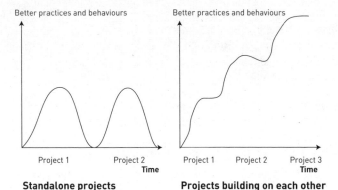

Better practices and behaviours

Project 1   Project 2
Time

Standalone projects

Better practices and behaviours

Project 1   Project 2   Project 3
Time

Projects building on each other

Figure 7.1 The consequences of projects being standalone or building on each other

By working in this way, people cannot ignore the new projects – they will not go away with time and so can no longer be ignored.

TIPS

- When building your team, find people who work well together but are not totally of the same mind. This way you will achieve consensus and come up with new ideas.
- You will have backstage activity, but involvement in decision making is important. Make sure that people do not think that too much is happening behind closed doors.
- You need to build the ability to change into the organization. Never give people the impression that this is the last change they will face. Use the change roles and team membership as vehicles for developing this skill.

Summary

If there is one message we want to leave you with at the end of this book, it is that change should be thought through and planned. Too many organizations leave change until it is too late, so keeping abreast of your organizational setting is essential to give you the time you need to adapt. Never believe that because your organization is performing well today, it will continue to do so into the future. It won't. But it is hard to change when things are seen as going well, so plan ahead and make people notice the warning signs.

Once the need for change has been agreed, plan your approach. You will have to respond to various crises and events as the change unfolds, but if you don't have an initial plan to guide you, you will be lost. So use the tools to decide your approach, identify resistance and steer the process. Ensure that the formal structures are in place and that there is both a change champion and a change manager for any major project.

Finally, change is now the rule, so treat those who lose out in the change process with respect. Organizations are judged by how they deal with their people. If it is done well, the next change will be easier to implement. If it is done badly, the next change will be harder, ossifying your organization and threatening its very survival.

SUNDAY

MONDAY

TUESDAY

WEDNESDAY

THURSDAY

FRIDAY

SATURDAY

Fact-check (answers at the back)

1. To avoid change, people will ...
   a) Argue why change isn't needed ☐
   b) Tell you why it won't work ☐
   c) Try to water down the change ☐
   d) Do all of the above ☐

2. When undertaking a change project, the original plan ...
   a) Should be stuck to rigidly ☐
   b) Should be ignored once the change starts ☐
   c) Is a guide, not a straitjacket ☐
   d) Is a waste of time ☐

3. During a change process, understanding the detail ...
   a) Is a distraction ☐
   b) Is important to ensure success ☐
   c) Diverts management effort from what is important ☐
   d) Is all of the above ☐

4. When senior managers give inconsistent messages by saying different things ...
   a) Staff become confused ☐
   b) Staff don't notice ☐
   c) Staff notice, but they ignore it ☐
   d) Staff don't care ☐

5. Senior management arguments over vision and strategy ...
   a) Never happen ☐
   b) Are the sign of weak management ☐
   c) Should be done publicly ☐
   d) Should be done backstage, in private ☐

6. Senior management arguments over vision and strategy are ...
   a) A waste of management time ☐
   b) Essential for the success of the business ☐
   c) Strongly discouraged ☐
   d) Damaging to the business ☐

7. A successful change will usually need ...
   a) A strong sponsor ☐
   b) A good project or change manager ☐
   c) A steering committee ☐
   d) All of the above ☐

8. The sponsor's role is to ...
   a) Manage the change ☐
   b) Manage the implementation ☐
   c) Champion the change ☐
   d) Do all of the above ☐

9. The change manager's role is to ...
   a) Manage the change ☐
   b) Manage the implementation ☐
   c) Report back problems and obstacles ☐
   d) Do all of the above ☐

10. Our main objective in writing this book is to ...
    a) Show you the tools available ☐
    b) Prescribe how you should manage change ☐
    c) Develop your skills ☐
    d) Help you think through change projects ☐

7 × 7

Seven quotations about change

People have been contemplating the need for change, and the difficulty in implementing it for centuries ...

1 'Progress is impossible without change, and those who cannot change their minds cannot change anything.' George Bernard Shaw

2 'You must be the change you wish to see in the world.' Mahatma Gandhi

3 'If you don't like something, change it. If you can't change it, change your attitude.' Maya Angelou

4 'It's not the strongest and most intelligent who will survive but those who can best manage change.' Charles Darwin

5 'They must often change who would be constant in happiness or wisdom.' Confucius

6 'I have noticed even people who claim everything is predestined, and that we can do nothing to change it, look before they cross the road.' Stephen Hawking

7 'There is nothing more difficult to take in hand, more perilous to conduct, or more uncertain in its success, than to take the lead in the introduction of a new order of things.' Niccolò Machiavelli

Seven tips for implanting change

1 Ensure that you have a goal and a compelling reason for change.
2 Create a plan and consider all the consequences.
3 Communicate – involve people in planning changes and be prepared to listen.
4 Take on board important points and be prepared to adapt provided you do not lose sight of your prime objective.
5 Create a time plan and regularly review progress.
6 Identify who is with you, who is against you and who is undecided, then act to change the balance in your favour.
7 Remember, planning and implementing change is not only an intellectual exercise; emotion is involved.

Seven pitfalls to be avoided

1 Not proceeding at an appropriate pace: too slow and you lose momentum; too fast and you leave people behind.
2 Thinking everyone sees the world as you do.
3 Believing that people are 'on side' when they are just paying lip service.
4 Believing only that others should change while you can remain as you are.
5 Not listening to the concerns of others: even if you can't allay their concerns, do them the courtesy of listening and considering what they have to say.
6 Not having the goal in sight – change is a means to an end not an end in itself.
7 Being too complacent – if it's too easy to be true, it's not true.

Seven tips for personal survival

Both for those implementing change and for those on the receiving end of change.

1 Change is tough, but remember that you are not alone; it's not a sign of weakness to feel under pressure but a sign that you understand the magnitude of the task.
2 Keep your work in perspective; external interests broaden your horizon and keep your mind fresh.
3 Don't overdo it. Look after your physical health – exercise and good eating habits help reduce stress and help you sleep. You won't be as effective if you are tired because you can't sleep.
4 Change causes anxiety and it's easy to imagine the worst. Spend a moment to think what 'the worst' would be (it may not be as bad as you think) and also what you could do to avoid it. Then consider whether there is any evidence the worst would actually happen.
5 Find someone to talk to – ideally someone outside your organization who can be objective.
6 Reinvent your job – create your own change before it is thrust on you.
7 If you are on the receiving end of change, be as objective as you can in considering what's happening. If, after all, you can't buy into it, move elsewhere and do it gracefully.

Seven trends that have changed our lives

Ponder for a moment changes that have taken place relatively recently ...

1 The Internet has completely changed the way we do business – from buying goods to researching information.
2 Mobile communication has spelled the end not only of iconic red telephone boxes but means that many people don't even have landlines in their homes.
3 Cheap and easy travel has led to widespread changes – from people buying second homes abroad to changes in what we eat and how we perceive other countries because we have been there.
4 Social media has subtly changed the balance of power between the company and the consumer.
5 Individual expression is seen as a right. People are looking for goods and services tailored to their needs.
6 Flexible working and working from home have become standard practice for many organizations – what does that mean for recruiting the best?
7 Attitude to debt has changed and may be changing again. Where once taking on an enormous mortgage was the norm for many people, it is now seen in the context of affordability. We have moved from saving to buy, to buying on credit, to a situation where banks have been blamed for lending too much money.

Seven company examples of change

1 Kodak – a great company that was synonymous with photographic film but which didn't embrace until too late the change to digital photography.
2 Blockbuster Video – managed the change from VHS to DVD but was caught out by the change to streaming.
3 Olivetti – built one of the first portable computers but still believed that typewriters were the future.
4 DEC – changed the market for mainframe computers by introducing its very successful range of mini-computers but was then itself overtaken by the move to microprocessors and networks
5 Nortel – in 2000 the ninth most valuable corporation in world, but went bankrupt just over a decade later when it focused solely on growth and lost sight of innovation and the market.
6 Leman Brothers – the fourth largest US investment bank survived the great depression of the 1930s but was brought down by their rush into subprime mortgages, so failed to recognize the changing environment and risks.
7 IBM – probably the world's most successful computer company; overtaken by technological change before reinventing itself as a provider of consulting services.

Seven mega-trends that will affect change in the future

No one has a crystal ball but the following trends appear likely ...

1 A move from monolithic sources of power to networks as technology allows smaller organizations to gain global presence.

2 Greater need for co-operation as nations become more co-dependent and businesses need to share ever-scarcer natural resources.

3 Growing population and urbanization will put pressure on infrastructure development.

4 Ageing populations will force new ways of thinking about, and funding, retirement, span and pattern of working life, and health care.

5 Environmental pressures and climate change cause governments to implement measures to bring about change in behaviour.

6 A move away from ownership to renting when required (this applies to houses as well as products such as cars).

7 Demographic and environmental pressures will stimulate development of disruptive technology, changing completely certain aspects of our lives. After all, it is said that 'Necessity is the mother of invention'.

Answers

Sunday: 1c; 2b; 3d; 4a; 5d; 6d; 7a; 8c; 9c; 10b

Monday: 1d; 2a; 3c; 4d; 5c; 6d; 7d; 8c 9c; 10d

Tuesday: 1c; 2c; 3c; 4a; 5c; 6b; 7d; 8b; 9b; 10d

Wednesday: 1d; 2b; 3d; 4a; 5c; 6a; 7d; 8d; 9b; 10b

Thursday: 1b; 2d; 3d; 4d; 5d; 6d; 7d; 8c; 9d; 10c

Friday: 1c; 2d; 3a; 4c; 5d; 6b; 7c; 8d; 9c; 10a

Saturday: 1d; 2c; 3b; 4a; 5d; 6b; 7d; 8c; 9d; 10d

Appendix: Checklist for change

Change is a complex process and trying to sum everything up into one final picture is extremely difficult. Below we have provided you with a checklist of some of the key questions and points to look out for. Our best advice is to use the tools and ideas from this book to think through your own situation and then to plan your own change. Remember, too, that not all change is possible so, if your analysis shows this, don't go blindly on. You do have a choice.

Questions to ask	What to watch out for
INITIAL CONCEPT	
• What change is required? • What are we trying to achieve? • What will be the benefits? • What will be the costs? • How long do we have to make the change? • What is the likelihood of success? • What are the alternatives? • What happens if we do not do it?	• Do not get tunnel vision – focus on outcomes and weigh carefully the possible alternatives for achieving them. • Do not underestimate obstacles. • Do not underestimate the power of entrenched personal interest.
UNFREEZING	
• Who will be on the project team(s)? • Who will be the change manager(s)? • What needs to be done and when? • What are the obstacles likely to be at each stage and how can they be overcome? • How will we create dissatisfaction with the present and paint a vision of the future? • What will be the milestones to show progress?	• Watch for disguised resistance – people saying 'yes' when they mean 'no', and actions not matching words. • Ensure that the task is not underestimated. • Do not under-allocate resources; change needs slack resource to be successfully implemented. • Watch the detail. • Ensure you create a sense of urgency.

(*Continued*)

Questions to ask	What to watch out for
MOVING	
• What are the indicators that change is happening? • Are new ways of working/ structure being adhered to? • Are the barriers being overcome? • Have significant dissenters been removed or neutralized? • Are people receiving sufficient support, coaching, training? • Do recognition and reward systems match what is being required by the change?	• Verify that changes are being made. • Create and celebrate quick wins. • Ensure that managers communicate a consistent message. • Handle sensitively those who genuinely can't handle the change. • Ensure that those who continue to resist the change leave the organization.
REFREEZING	
• Is the recognition and reward system continuing to support the change? • Have new ways of working become part of the routine? • Has the change delivered the expected benefits? • What needs to be changed next?	• Check that people are not sliding back into old ways of working. • Continually monitor performance. • Do not celebrate victory too early. • Ensure that benefits are being delivered and communicated.

Acknowledgements

The authors would like to thank the Engineering and Physical Science Research Council, whose grant informed this work, and the following people and organizations for the use of their illustrations in this publication:

Figure 3.1, Carnall 1995, reprinted by permission of Pearson Education Limited, England. Figures 3.2 and 3.3, Connor 1992, reprinted by permission of Organizational Development Resources, England.

Although the cases included in this book are based on real life, they have been disguised to protect those involved. It should also be noted that, in places, cases have been combined to make specific points, and so no connections should be made to any real people or organizations.

Every effort has been made to trace the copyright for material used in this book. The authors and publishers would be happy to make arrangements with any holder of copyright whom it has not been possible to trace by the time of going to press.